CAMBRIDGE
UNIVERSITY PRESS

CAMBRIDGE Primary Mathematics

Learner's Book 3

Cherri Moseley & Janet Rees

CAMBRIDGE
UNIVERSITY PRESS

University Printing House, Cambridge CB2 8BS, United Kingdom

One Liberty Plaza, 20th Floor, New York, NY 10006, USA

477 Williamstown Road, Port Melbourne, VIC 3207, Australia

314–321, 3rd Floor, Plot 3, Splendor Forum, Jasola District Centre, New Delhi – 110025, India

103 Penang Road, #05-06/07, Visioncrest Commercial, Singapore 238467

Cambridge University Press is part of the University of Cambridge.

It furthers the University's mission by disseminating knowledge in the pursuit of education, learning and research at the highest international levels of excellence.

www.cambridge.org
Information on this title: www.cambridge.org/9781108746489

First published 2014
Second edition 2021

20 19

Printed in Malaysia by Vivar Printing

A catalogue record for this publication is available from the British Library

ISBN 978-1-108-74648-9 Paperback with Digital Access (1 Year)
ISBN 978-1-108-96413-5 Digital Learner's Book (1 Year)
ISBN 978-1-108-96415-9 Learner's Book eBook

Additional resources for this publication at www.cambridge.org/go

Projects and their accompanying teacher guidance have been written by the NRICH Team. NRICH is an innovative collaboration between the Faculties of Mathematics and Education at the University of Cambridge, which focuses on problem solving and on creating opportunities for students to learn mathematics through exploration and discussion **https://nrich.maths.org**.

Introduction

Welcome to Stage 3 of Cambridge Primary Mathematics. We hope that this book will show you how interesting and exciting mathematics can be.

Mathematics is everywhere. Everyone uses mathematics every day. Where have you noticed mathematics?

Have you ever wondered about any of these questions?

- What can I do to help me make good estimates of quantities?
- What is the complement of a number?
- How are multiplication and division connected?
- What is an equivalent fraction?
- What do 'kilo', 'centi' and 'milli' mean?
- What are area and perimeter? How are they the same? How are they different?
- How do you read a timetable?
- What is a right angle?
- How can I explain to someone how to get to the park?
- How do you solve a mathematics problem?

You will work like a mathematician to find the answers to some of these questions. It is good to talk about the mathematics as you explore, sharing ideas. You will reflect on what you did and how you did it, and think about whether you would do the same next time.

You will be able to practise new skills and check how you are doing and also challenge yourself to find out more. You will be able to make connections between what seem to be different areas of mathematics.

We hope you enjoy thinking and working like a mathematician.

Cherri Moseley and Janet Rees

Contents

How to use this book

In this book you will find lots of different features to help your learning:

Questions to find out what you know already. →

Getting started

1 Shapes can be grouped using their faces, vertices or edges.

Draw arrows to sort these shapes into a group.
Some will go into more than one group.

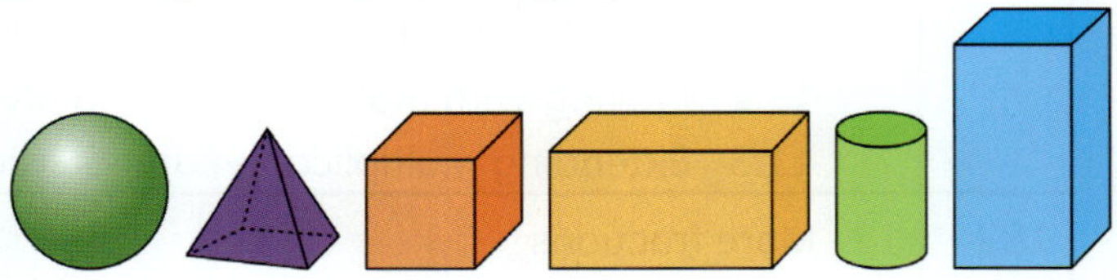

one or more curved surfaces	all faces rectangular	more than five vertices

What you will learn in the unit. →

We are going to ...

- learn about prisms and find what is the same and what is different between prisms and pyramids
- build and name 3D shapes
- describe and sketch 3D shapes.

Important words that you will use. →

buy change
decimal point
money notation
spend

Step-by-step examples showing a way to solve a problem. →

Worked example 1

What is the value of the ringed digit in this 3-digit number?

4⑦2

472 is four hundred and seventy-two.	It helps to say the number out loud.
The 7 is in the tens place.	You say the value of each digit as you read it.
The value of the 7 is 7 tens, so it is 70.	

These questions will help you develop your skills of thinking and working mathematically.

> 7 Explain what happens to a single-digit number and a 2-digit number when it is multiplied by 10.

An investigation to carry out with a partner or in groups. Where this icon appears the activity will help develop your skills of thinking and working mathematically.

> **Think like a mathematician**
>
> Tomas made nine 3-digit numbers using a set of place value cards. Seven of the numbers are 473, 689, 358, 134, 925, 247 and 791. What could the other two numbers be?
>
> Compare your numbers with those of someone else in your class.
>
> If your numbers are different, can you explain why?

Questions to help you think about how you learn.

> *Arun says multiples of 10 are special numbers. Why do you think Arun says that?*

What you have learned in the unit.

> **Look what I can do!**
>
> - [ ] I can read and record time using analogue clocks.
> - [ ] I can read and record time using digital clocks.
> - [ ] I can link analogue and digital times.

Questions that cover what you have learned in the unit.

> **Check your progress**
>
> 1 Complete these pieces, which are from a 1 to 1000 number grid.

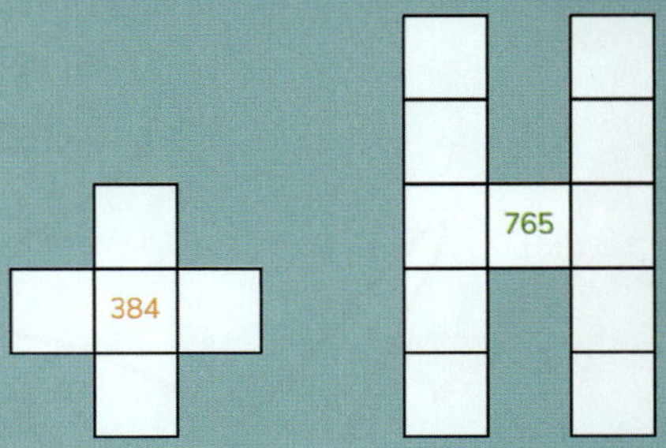

At the end of several units, there is a project for you to carry out using what you have learned. You might make something or solve a problem.

Project 4

> **Dicey fractions**
>
> Sofia and Arun are playing a fraction game. They draw a grid like this and write a denominator of 10 in each box:

$\frac{}{10}$	$\frac{}{10}$	$\frac{}{10}$
$\frac{}{10}$	$\frac{}{10}$	$\frac{}{10}$
$\frac{}{10}$	$\frac{}{10}$	$\frac{}{10}$

Projects and their accompanying teacher guidance have been written by the NRICH Team. NRICH is an innovative collaboration between the Faculties of Mathematics and Education at the University of Cambridge, which focuses on problem solving and on creating opportunities for students to learn mathematics through exploration and discussion. nrich.maths.org.

Thinking and Working Mathematically

There are some important skills that you will develop as you learn mathematics.

Specialising is when I choose an example and check to see if it satisfies or does not satisfy specific mathematical criteria.

Characterising is when I identify and describe the mathematical properties of an object.

Generalising is when I recognise an underlying pattern by identifying many examples that satisfy the same mathematical criteria.

Classifying is when I organise objects into groups according to their mathematical properties.

Critiquing is when I compare and evaluate mathematical ideas, representations or solutions to identify advantages and disadvantages.

Improving is when I refine mathematical ideas or representations to develop a more effective approach or solution.

Conjecturing is when I form mathematical questions or ideas.

Convincing is when I present evidence to justify or challenge a mathematical idea or solution.

1 Numbers to 1000

Getting started

1 Complete the 100 square pieces.

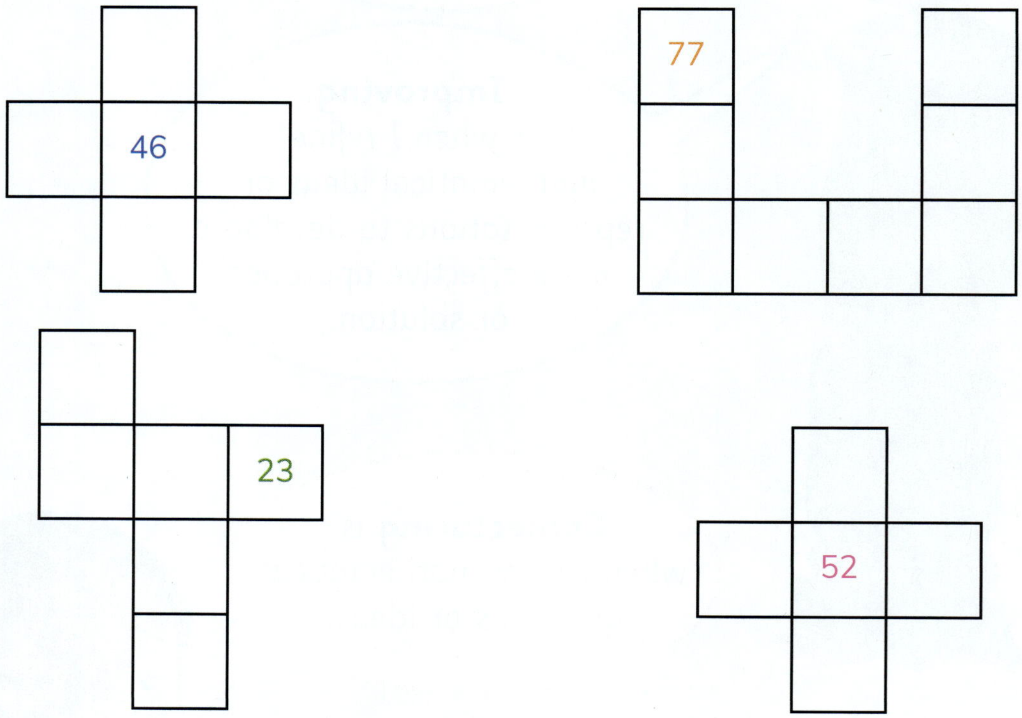

2 Mark 42 and 87 on the number line.

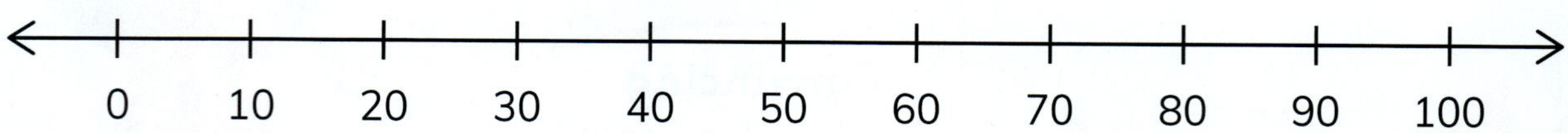

3 Round each number to the nearest 10.

72 ☐ 29 ☐ 45 ☐ 60 ☐

We all use numbers every day. In this unit you will explore numbers to 1000. There are 365 days in a year, you might live at number 321 or read a book with 180 pages in it.

1.1 Hundreds, tens and ones

We are going to ...

- say, read and write numbers and number words from 0 to 1000
- know the value of each digit in a 3-digit number
- count on and count back in steps of 1 and 10 from any number.

3-digit numbers are made up of hundreds, tens and ones.

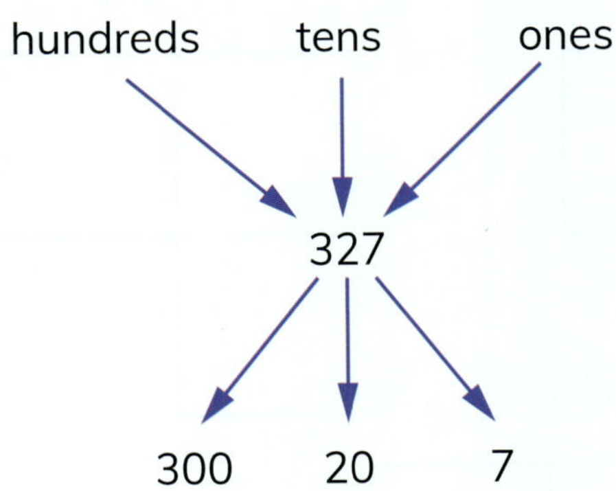

thousand

You need to know what each digit represents to understand the value of the whole number.

Exercise 1.1

1 Complete these pieces, which are from a 1 to 1000 number strip.

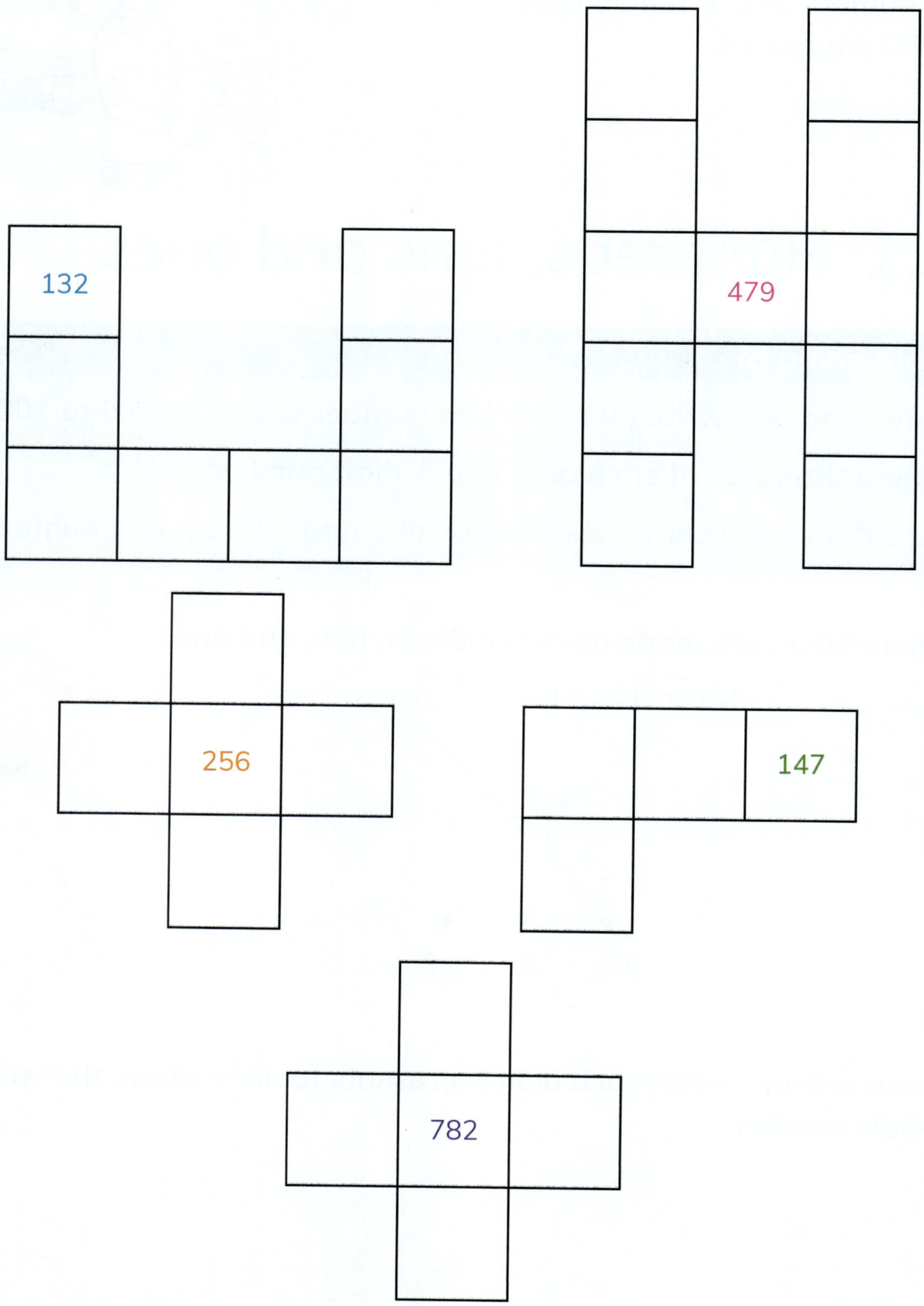

2 Complete the missing numbers.

428 = ☐00 + ☐0 + ☐

913 = ☐00 + ☐0 + ☐

☐ ☐ ☐ = 500 + 70 + 6

☐ ☐ ☐ = 300 + 90 + 5

3 What 3-digit number is shown in each place value grid?

a

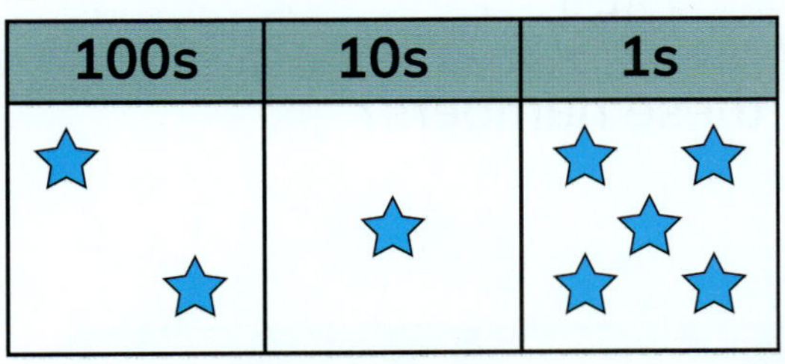

☐

b

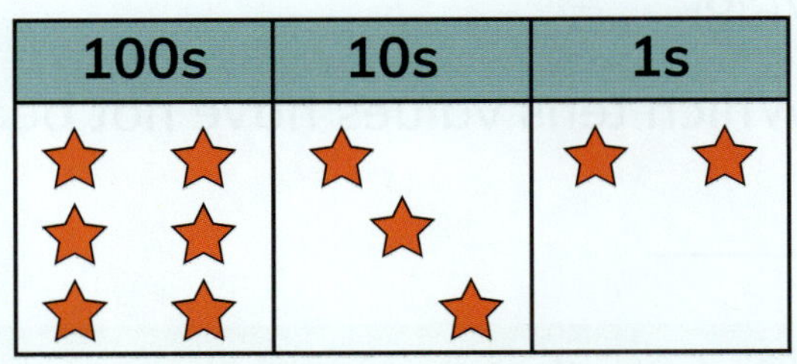

☐

4 What 3-digit number is represented below?

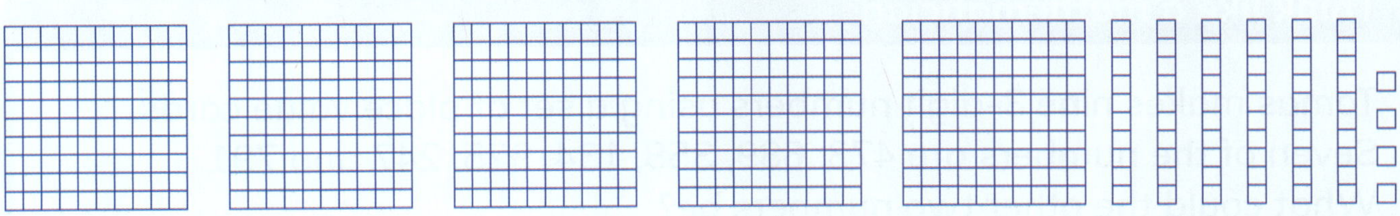

☐

Worked example 1

What is the value of the ringed digit in this 3-digit number?

4⑦2

472 is four hundred and seventy-two.

The 7 is in the tens place.

The value of the 7 is 7 tens, so it is 70.

It helps to say the number out loud.

You say the value of each digit as you read it.

5 What is the value of the ringed digit in each 3-digit number?

6③7 ____________ 10⑨ ____________

⑨21 ____________ 3⑨4 ____________

76⑧ ____________ ②53 ____________

Which tens values have not been used in these numbers?

______

Is it easier to find the value of the hundreds, tens or ones digit? Why do you think that is?

Think like a mathematician

Tomas makes nine 3-digit numbers using a set of place value cards. Seven of the numbers are 473, 689, 358, 134, 925, 247 and 791. What could the other two numbers be?

Compare your numbers with those of someone else in your class.

If your numbers are different, can you explain why?

6 Use these number words to write four 3-digit numbers in words.

hundred	eight	and	seventy-	fifty-	three

1 ____________________

2 ____________________

3 ____________________

4 ____________________

Look what I can do!

- ☐ I can say, read and write numbers and number words from 0 to 1000.
- ☐ I know the value of each digit in a 3-digit number.
- ☐ I can count on and count back in steps of 1 and 10 from any number.

1.2 Comparing and ordering

We are going to ...

- compare numbers by looking at the value of each digit in turn
- use the inequality symbols is less than, <, and is greater than, >, when comparing two numbers
- order numbers from smallest to greatest and from greatest to smallest.

When you know the value of each digit in a 3-digit number, you can compare numbers and use what you find out to put them in order. You can also estimate where a number belongs on the number line.

digit
inequality
inequalities
is greater than, >
is less than, <
symbol

Exercise 1.2

1 Complete these pieces from a 1000 square.

2 Compare these numbers and complete the sentences.

a

100s	10s	1s
4	5	8
6	4	3

________ is greater than ________

and ________ is less than ________.

b

100s	10s	1s
4	7	5
4	7	2

________ is greater than ________

and ________ is less than ________.

c

100s	10s	1s
8	3	8
8	8	3

________ is greater than ________

and ________ is less than ________.

3 Order these numbers from smallest to greatest.

679 475 621 38 563

smallest greatest

4 Order these numbers from greatest to smallest.

48 834 438 384 483

______ ______ ______ ______ ______

greatest smallest

5 Mark the numbers in question 4 on the number line.

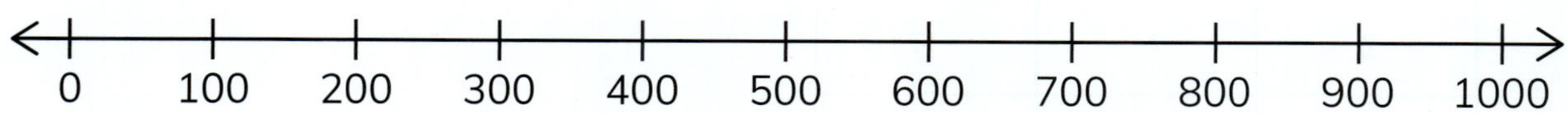

6 Estimate the value of each number marked on the number line.

Tip

Remember that 'estimate' means a sensible guess.

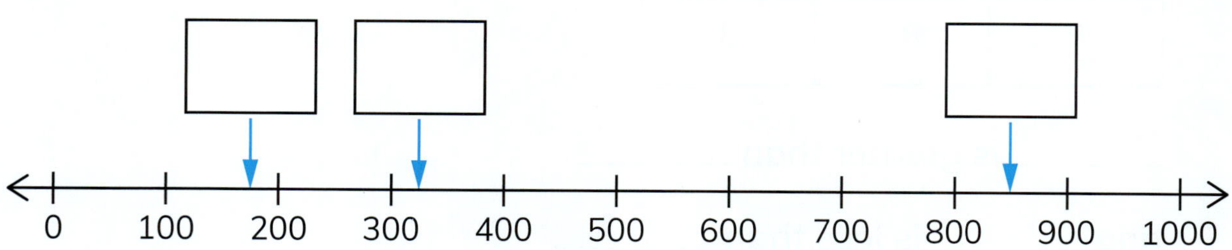

7 Complete these inequalities.

______ < 263 671 < ______

______ > 457 346 > ______

Think like a mathematician

Use these numbers and symbols to make three correct statements.

234, 243, 243, 278, 278, 287, <, =, >.

Find a different way to do it.

Compare your answers with those of someone else in your class. How are they the same? How are they different? Work together to find all the possible solutions.

Do you agree with Sofia? Why?

Look what I can do!

- ☐ I can compare numbers by looking at the value of each digit in turn.
- ☐ I can use the inequality symbols is less than, <, and is greater than, >, when comparing two numbers.
- ☐ I can order numbers from smallest to greatest and from greatest to smallest.

1.3 Estimating and rounding

We are going to ...

- estimate quantities by giving a range of numbers as an estimate
- round numbers to the nearest 10
- round numbers to the nearest 100.

You don't always need to know how many there are. Often, an estimate is enough. You can estimate by giving a range of numbers or by rounding a number to the nearest 10 or 100.

estimate
range
round, rounding

Exercise 1.3

1 Estimate how many spots there are in the box.

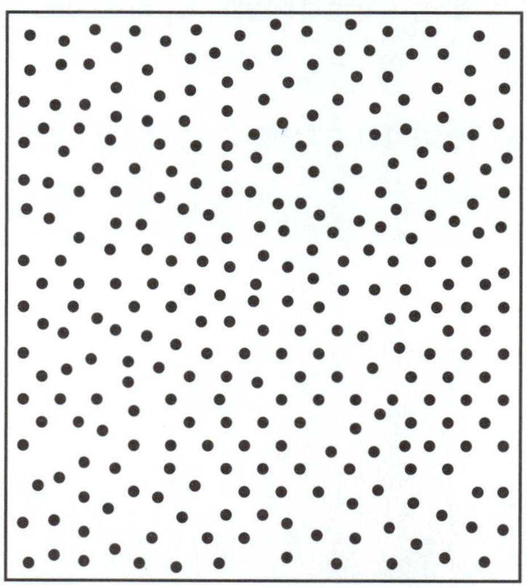

2 Class 3 use this table to check their estimates of the number of beans in different containers.

Number of beans	Mass of beans
100	10 grams
200	20 grams
300	30 grams
400	40 grams
500	50 grams
600	60 grams
700	70 grams
800	80 grams
900	90 grams
1000	100 grams

a Marcus estimates that his bowl has 400 to 500 beans.

They weigh 56 grams. Is this a good estimate? ________

b Zara estimates that her plastic bag has 200 to 300 beans.

They weigh 24 grams. Is this a good estimate? ________

c Arun's beans weigh 78 grams.

What range would be a good estimate for his beans? ________

3 Round each number to the nearest 10.

123		678		385	
907		740		598	

4 Round each number to the nearest 100.

123		678		385	
907		740		598	

If the numbers in questions 3 and 4 were dollars ($), grams or kilometres, could you round them to the nearest 10 or 100 dollars ($), grams or kilometres?

5 Which number in questions 3 and 4 rounds to the same number when rounded to the nearest 10 and to the nearest 100?

Think like a mathematician

When a number is rounded to the nearest 10 and the same number is rounded to the nearest 100, the answer is the same. What could the number be?

Sofia includes 100, 200, 300, 400, 500, 600, 700, 800, 900 and 1000 in her list of numbers. Do you agree with her? Why?

Look what I can do!

- ☐ I can estimate quantities by giving a range of numbers as an estimate.
- ☐ I can round numbers to the nearest 10.
- ☐ I can round numbers to the nearest 100.

Check your progress

1 Complete these pieces, which are from a 1 to 1000 number strip.

2 What is the value of the ringed digit in each 3-digit number?

56⑦ ____________ ⑦29 ____________

6⑦4 ____________ 92③ ____________

⑧88 ____________ 4④4 ____________

3 Write the missing numbers.

Number	Round to the nearest 10	Round to the nearest 100
234		
471		
896		
750		
303		
987		

2 Statistics: Tally charts and frequency tables

Getting started

1 Complete this chart by using tally marks to record how many animals are in the zoo.

giraffes 7 lions 4 camels 6 meerkats 15 fish 26

penguins 17 seals 5

Animal	Tally

How do you find things out? Often, you ask a question and then find a way to gather information to answer it. This is what Statistics is all about.

This unit looks at how you can record the information you gather. In this picture, the children want to find out how many of each animal there are in the zoo. What are they using to record the data?

2.1 Tally charts and frequency tables

We are going to ...

- conduct investigations to answer non-statistical and statistical questions
- record, organise and represent data using a tally chart and a frequency table
- describe data and discuss conclusions.

You are planning a party for your class. You want to know what drinks to order. What question could you ask?

What is your favourite drink?

You could record your data in a tally chart. Tally charts are used to collect data quickly.

A tally chart uses marks. The marks are grouped in fives.

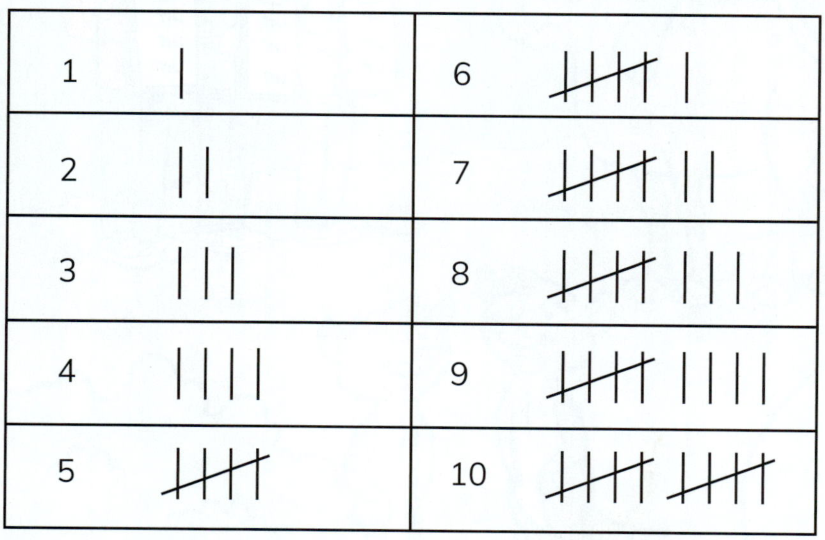

frequency table
survey

Once your tally chart is complete, you could make a frequency table. A frequency table uses a number to show how many times something occurs. This makes it easy to read because you do not need to count the tally marks each time.

Favourite drink	Tally	Frequency
water	卌 ||	7
milkshake	卌 ||||	9

What does your frequency table show you?

What drinks will you order for the party?

Worked example 1

If you throw a dice 12 times, how many times do you think each number will appear?

I think the dice will land on each number twice.

Your idea about what you think will happen is called a conjecture.

Throw the dice 12 times.
Use tally marks to record the results of each throw.

For example:

<table>
<tr><th>1</th><th>2</th><th>3</th><th>4</th><th>5</th><th>6</th></tr>
<tr><td>|||</td><td>|||</td><td>||</td><td>|</td><td>|</td><td>||</td></tr>
</table>

The dice has not landed on each number twice, so your conjecture is wrong.

These are chance throws, so there will be more than one answer each time you do this activity.

Now try it yourself and compare your results with a partner's results.

1	2	3	4	5	6

Exercise 2.1

1 You will need a coin.

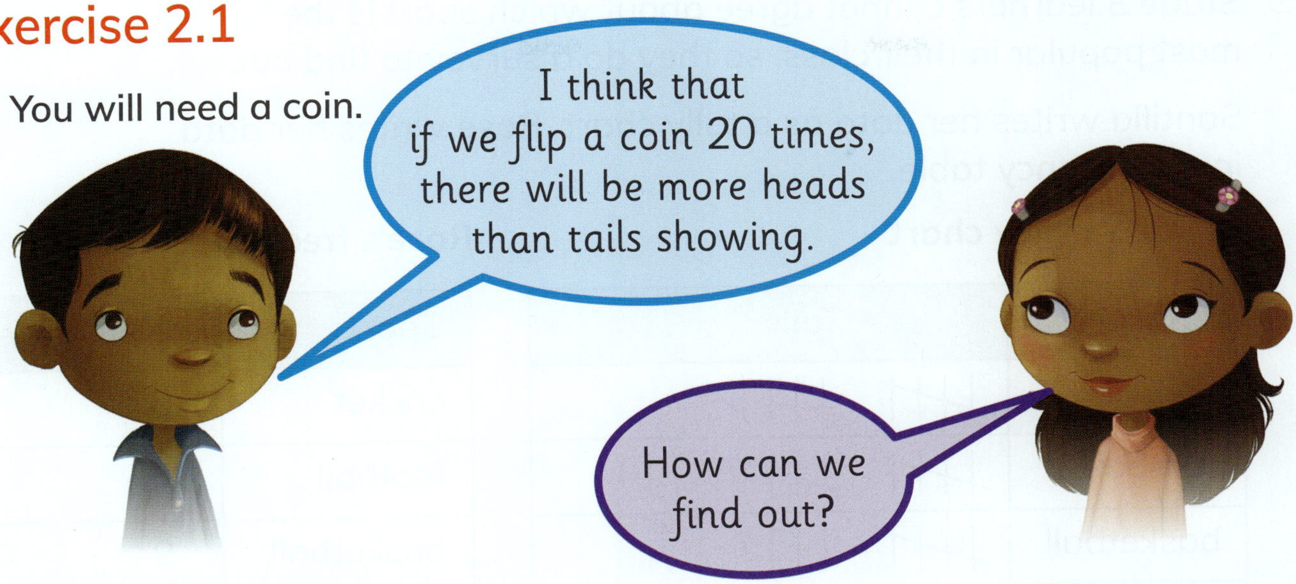

Flip the coin 20 times.

Use tally marks to show the results of heads or tails.

Heads	Tails

Write two things that you have found out using the data in the tally chart.

1 ____________________

2 ____________________

You can count each result and you can compare the results.

Do you think that the same thing will happen if you repeat the activity? Explain what you think.

____

____

2 Stage 3 learners cannot agree about which sport is the most popular in their class, so they do a survey to find out.

Santilla writes her data as a tally chart. Rose writes her data in a frequency table.

Santilla's tally chart

Sport	Tally
cricket	卌 ||||
football	卌 卌 ||||
basketball	卌 ||||
swimming	卌 卌 ||
running	卌 |

Rose's frequency table

Sport	Frequency
cricket	9
football	14
basketball	9
swimming	12
running	6

Discuss with a partner how the two tables are different.
Do they both record the same data?
What are the advantages and disadvantages of each table?

a Which sport is liked the most? ______________________

b Which two sports are liked by the same number of people?

____

c How many people took part in the survey? ______________________

d Write two things that the data does not tell you.

1 ____

2 ____

3

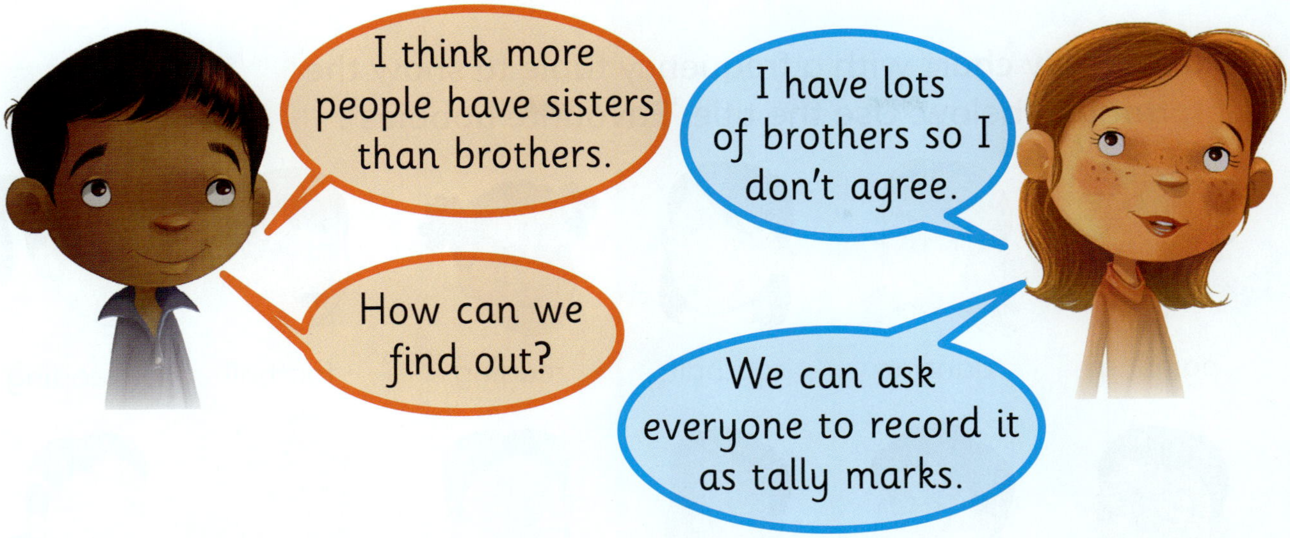

Complete the table by asking the children in your class how many sisters and brothers they have.

	Brothers	Sisters	Total tally	Frequency
0				
1				
2				
3				
4				
5				
6				

Write four things that the table shows you about your data.

1 ____

2 ____

3 ____

4 ____

4 Make a tally chart with a frequency table to show the information below. Use the title 'Favourite hobbies'.

a How many children chose painting as their favourite hobby? ______

b What is the most popular hobby? ____________

c What is the least favourite hobby? ____________

d Discuss with a partner.
You are helping to organise an after-school club.
How could the information from the tally chart and frequency table help you?
What other things would you want to find out?

Think like a mathematician

Work with a partner.

A cereal company is offering six free gifts.
One gift appears in every cereal packet.

How many packets do you think you would need to buy so that you have all of the gifts?

If you did this investigation again, would you do it in the same way or do something different?

If you did this investigation again, would the results be the same? How will you know which is the true result?

Look what I can do!

- [ ] I can conduct investigations to answer non-statistical and statistical questions.
- [ ] I can record, organise and represent data using a tally chart and a frequency table.
- [ ] I can describe data and discuss conclusions.

Check your progress

1 Use the chart to answer the questions.

Number of learners in the class

First week	Second week	Third week	Fourth week
卌 卌 卌 ||||	卌 卌 卌 ||	卌 卌 卌 卌 ||	卌 卌 卌

a In which week is the number of learners more than 20?

____

b Add the number of learners in the second and fourth week together. What is the total?

____

c How many more learners were present in the first week than in the fourth week?

____

2 Complete the chart to show the tally marks for this data.

- 12 people like apple.
- Double that amount like mango.
- Grapes are liked by half the number of those who like apple.
- Bananas are liked most by seven people.

Fruit	Tally
mango	
apple	
grape	
banana	

How many people took part in the survey?

____

Continued

3 This table shows learners' scores from a maths test.

40	90	30	90	40	60	30	80
60	60	80	50	40	80	40	80
50	70	80	90	90	80	40	70

Use the data to complete the table.

Score	Tally	Frequency
30		
40		
50		
60		
70		
80		
90		

Write three things that the table shows you.

1 ____

2 ____

3 ____

3 Addition, subtraction and money

Getting started

1 The addition machine adds 43 to each number in the grid. Complete the answer grid. How will you find your totals?

11	25	13
32	56	34
46	21	40

2 Choose a number from the second jar of numbers to subtract from a number in the first jar. How will you find your answers?

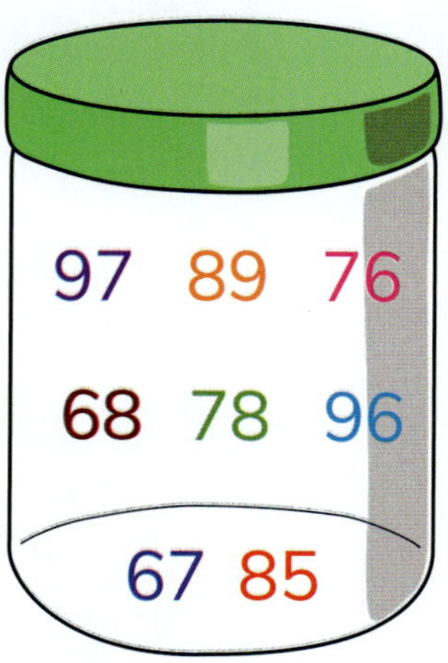

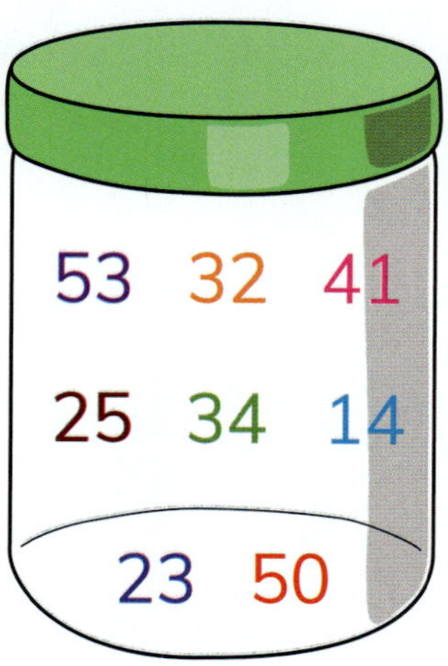

Continued

3 Bruno buys a T-shirt for US$16 and 95c.
Which banknotes and coins could he pay with?

Find a different way to pay.

You add and subtract every day for lots of different reasons. You also add and subtract with money to find out if you have enough money to buy things and how much change you will get.

3.1 Addition

We are going to ...

- add a 3-digit number and a single-digit number, regrouping the ones
- estimate and add a 3-digit number and a 2-digit number, regrouping the ones
- estimate and add two 3-digit numbers, regrouping the ones.

You can already add two 2-digit numbers.
In this unit you will find out how to add numbers with up to three digits. You will find out what to do when you have too many ones for the ones place.

compose
decompose
exchange
regroup
single

Exercise 3.1

1 Choose one number from each number jar to add together. Show your method. Do this three times.

2 Read across the grid or down the grid to find a 3-digit number. Then choose a single digit from any square in the grid to add to your number.

Show your method. Do this three times.

5	1	2
3	6	8
4	7	9

3 On Tuesday, 134 adults and 53 children visited the library. How many people visited the library on Tuesday?

Estimate and then find the total. Show your method.

Tip

Round each number to the nearest 10 to help you estimate your answer.

4 On Thursday, 215 adults and 67 children visited the museum. How many people visited the museum on Thursday?

Estimate and then find the total.
Show your method.

5 A baker makes 148 chocolate cakes and 136 lemon cakes.

How many cakes has the baker made?
Estimate then calculate.
Show your method.

6 The school library has 439 fiction books and 326 non-fiction books.

How many books does the library have altogether? Estimate then calculate.
Show your method.

Think like a mathematician

Kiko spilt some ink on the ones digits in her calculation.

24 + 13 = 381

What could her calculation have been?

Did you find all the possibilities for Kiko's calculation?

Compare your solutions with those of other learners in your class.

Complete the sentence. Next time, when I investigate a calculation like Kiko's, I will ...

Look what I can do!

- ☐ I can add a 3-digit number and a single-digit number, regrouping the ones.
- ☐ I can estimate and add a 3-digit number and a 2-digit number, regrouping the ones.
- ☐ I can estimate and add two 3-digit numbers, regrouping the ones.

3.2 Subtraction

We are going to ...

- subtract a single-digit number from a 3-digit number, regrouping to get enough ones
- estimate and subtract a 2-digit number from a 3-digit number, regrouping to get enough ones
- estimate and subtract a 3-digit number from a 3-digit number, regrouping to get enough ones.

You can already subtract a 2-digit number from another 2-digit number. In this section you will find out how to subtract a 1-, 2- or 3-digit number from a 3-digit number. You will find out what to do if you don't have enough ones to subtract from.

Exercise 3.2

1 Use the three digits 4, 6 and 8 to make a 2-digit number and a 1-digit number. Subtract the single-digit number from the 2-digit number. Show your method.

Can you find and solve the six possible calculations?

4 6 8

2 Use the four digits 3, 5, 7 and 9 to make a 3-digit number and a 1-digit number. Subtract the single-digit number from the 3-digit number. Show your method.

Find and solve at least six of the possible calculations.

3 5 7 9

3 178 cartons of milk are delivered to the store. 25 of them are damaged.

How many cartons of milk can the store sell? Estimate then calculate. Show your method.

4 262 melons are delivered to the store, but 37 of them are damaged.

How many melons can the store sell? Estimate then calculate. Show your method.

5 On Tuesday, the post office has 472 parcels for delivery.
A van takes 267 of the parcels.

How many parcels are still at the post office?
Estimate then calculate. Show your method.

6 On Friday, the post office has 683 parcels for delivery.
A van takes 548.

How many parcels are still at the post office?
Estimate then calculate. Show your method.

Think like a mathematician

Faisal spilt some ink on the ones digits in his calculation.

49■ – 14■ = 345

What could his calculation have been?

Did you find all the possibilities for Faisal's calculation?

Compare your solutions with those of other learners in your class.

How is exploring a subtraction like Faisal's the same as exploring an addition like Kiko's in Section 3.1?
How is it different?
Discuss with your partner or in a small group.

Look what I can do!

- ☐ I can subtract a single-digit number from a 3-digit number, regrouping to get enough ones.
- ☐ I can estimate and subtract a 2-digit number from a 3-digit number, regrouping to get enough ones.
- ☐ I can estimate and subtract a 3-digit number from a 3-digit number, regrouping to get enough ones.

3.3 Money

We are going to ...

- use the decimal point to show two different units of money in the same amount
- add amounts of money and use this to find the change
- subtract amounts of money to find the change.

Adding and subtracting money is the same as adding and subtracting numbers. You must make sure that you take note of the currency units when you add and subtract. $5 – 5c does not leave you with no money!

buy change
decimal point
money notation
spend

Exercise 3.3

Worked example

How do I use a decimal point to record $4 and 24c?

$4 and 24c	The number of dollars is written after the dollar sign ($), before the decimal point. The number of cents is written after the decimal point.
= $4.24	The dollar sign tells you it is money, so you don't need to use the c for cents as well.

1 Write each amount using a decimal point.

Using dollars and cents	Using a decimal point
$4 and 50c	
$8 and 70c	
$24 and 5c	
$10	
$0 and 99c	

2 How many dollars and cents are there in each of these amounts?

Using dollars and cents	Using a decimal point
	$20.45
	$9.75
	$15
	$2.09
	$0.30

3 Use a decimal point to write each amount of money in dollars and cents.

a

____

b 

____

c 

____

d 

____

The 1c coin costs more than 1c to make. Some people think that it should no longer be made and used. What do you think? Discuss with your partner or in a small group.

Think like a mathematician

Zara has two different banknotes and two different coins in her pocket.

How much money could she have?

What is the greatest amount of money that she could have?

What is the smallest amount of money that she could have?

4 Some children visit the school shop. The price of each item is shown.

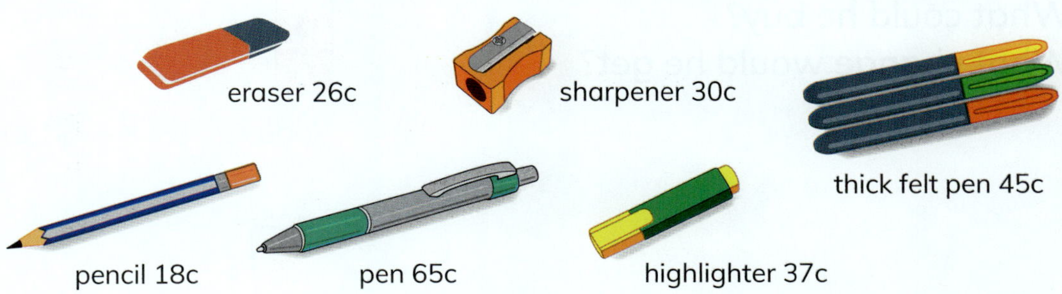

a Sumi has 50c. She buys a pencil and an eraser.
How much does she spend? How much change will she have?

b Virun has 90c. He buys two highlighter pens.
How much does he spend? How much change will he have?

c Alicija has 75c. She buys two items and has 12c change.
What does she buy? Find two different answers.

5 a Jamila buys a coffee, a soda and a milkshake with $10.
How much does she spend?
How much change will she get?

b Liam has $5 to spend on two drinks.
He does not like coffee.
What could he buy?
What change would he get?

Drinks Menu

Coffee $3

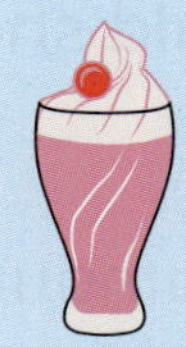

Milkshake $3 and 25c

Tea $2

Soda $1 and 10c

Orange juice $2 and 20c

6 Two ice creams cost $8. How much does one ice cream cost?

Write your number sentence and solve it to find the cost of an ice cream.

7 Priya pays for her trainers with a $50 note. She gets $17 change. How much do the trainers cost?

Write your number sentence and solve it to find the cost of the trainers.

8 Xiumin has $6 and 50c. He buys a comic and gets $1 and 20c change. How much does the comic cost?

Write your number sentence and solve it to find the cost of the comic.

9 Isha writes the calculation $50 – 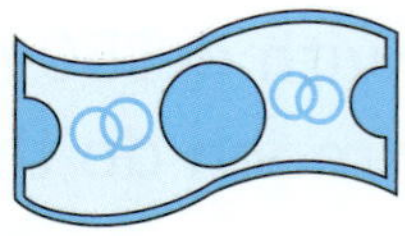 = $21.

Write a word problem to match Isha's number sentence.

Look what I can do!

- ☐ I can use the decimal point to show the two different units of money in an amount.
- ☐ I can add amounts of money and use this to find the change.
- ☐ I can subtract amounts of money to find the change.

Check your progress

1 A baker makes 147 lemon cakes and 225 fruit cakes.
How many cakes does the baker make? Estimate then calculate.
Show your method.

2 384 children visit the museum on a school day.
At 3 o'clock in the afternoon, 158 children return to school.
How many children are still at the museum?
Estimate and then find the answer. Show your method.

Continued

3 Bao pays for his new jacket with a $50 note.
He gets $24 change. How much does the jacket cost?
Write your number sentence and solve it to find the cost of the jacket.

Project 1

Surprising sums

Marcus explores the digit sums of different numbers. He knows that to find the digit sum of a number, he has to add the digits together. If the answer isn't a 1-digit number, Marcus will add the digits of this number, repeating this until his final answer is a 1-digit number.

For example, to find the digit sum of 76, Marcus would start by calculating 7 + 6 = 13. Then because 13 isn't a 1-digit number he would work out 1 + 3 = 4. As 4 is a 1-digit number, this is the digit sum of 76.

He starts with the number 435.

What steps does Marcus go through to find the digit sum?

Does the digit sum of this number give us any information about the number 435?

In his maths lesson, Marcus is practising 2-digit addition. He works out that 22 + 41 = 63. He is curious about how the digit sum changes when you add two numbers together, so he works out the digit sums of 22 and 41, and then he finds the digit sum of 63.

Have a go at working out these digit sums. What do you notice?

Marcus also knows that 45 + 24 = 69, and he works out the digit sums of these three numbers.

Continued

What do you notice this time? How are the digit sums of 45 and 24 related to the digit sum of 69?

Have a go at making up an addition question and answering it. You can then find the digit sums of all the numbers you have used.

Do you notice anything? If so, what?

What happens if we add more than two numbers together?

What happens if we add bigger numbers together?

Do you think the patterns you have spotted will always work? Why or why not?

4 3D shapes

Getting started

1 Shapes can be grouped using their faces, vertices or edges.

Draw arrows to sort these shapes into a group.
Some will go into more than one group.

one or more curved surfaces

all faces rectangular

more than five vertices

2 Name two 3D shapes that have fewer than six vertices.

This unit will introduce you to prisms. You will compare prisms and pyramids to find what is the same and what is different about them. You will use what you know about 3D shapes to identify, build, name, describe and sketch them.

Cereal
CEREAL
Fresh
Lemon
Juice
biscuits
Pineapple
Juice

What 3D shapes can you see in the picture? Try creating the shapes with blocks or other objects.

4.1 3D shapes

We are going to ...

- learn about prisms and find what is the same and what is different between prisms and pyramids
- build and name 3D shapes
- describe and sketch 3D shapes.

You will have seen 3D shapes all around you but do you know what they are? Do you know what a prism is? Can you find prisms at school and at home?

This section will help you to recognise prisms and pyramids and use other more familiar 3D shapes in different puzzles and activities.

apex
prism

Worked example 1

A prism has two ends that are the same shape and size.
It has flat faces.

Which shapes are **not** prisms?

a 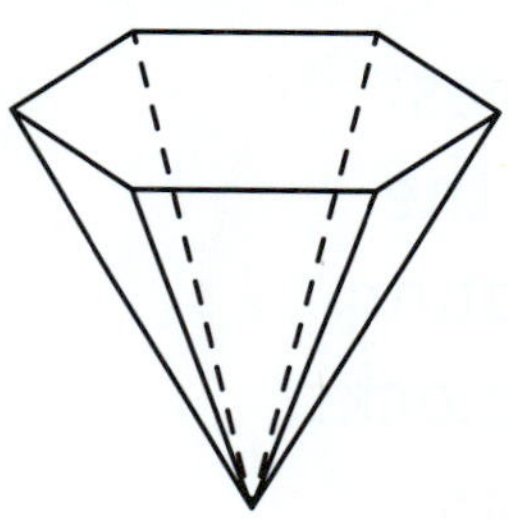
b 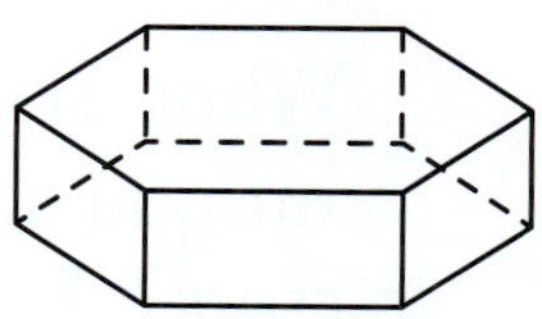
c 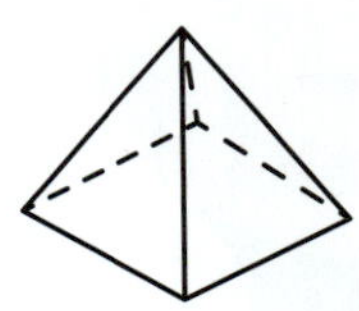
d 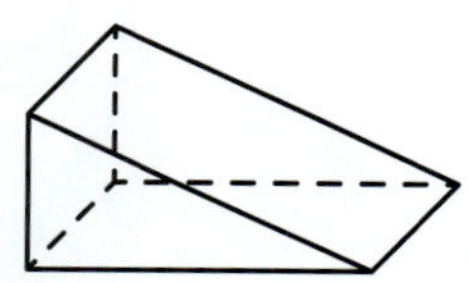

e 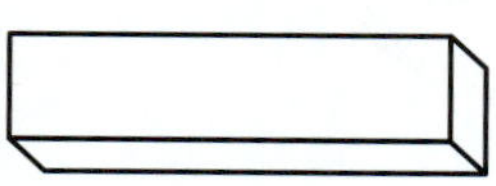
f 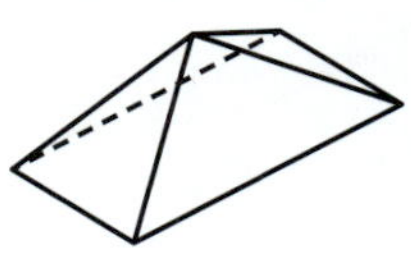
g 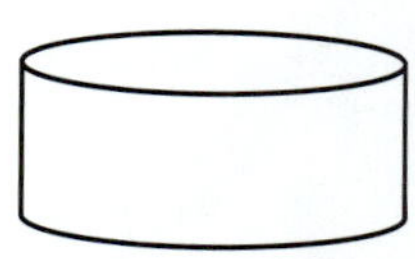

Look at the ends. Look at the faces.

a, **c**, **f** and **g** are not prisms because they do not all have flat faces or two ends that are the same shape and size.

Exercise 4.1

1 Sort the shapes. Join them with a line.

Curved edges | Straight edges

Now write your own labels.

Use a different colour to draw the lines and sort the shapes in a different way.

Sketch 2 3D shapes for each of your rules.

2 Work with a partner.

Choose six different 3D shapes.

Decide what criteria you will use to sort your shapes using a Venn diagram.

Label the circles in the Venn diagram.

Draw or write the names of the shapes in the correct part of the diagram.

3D shapes

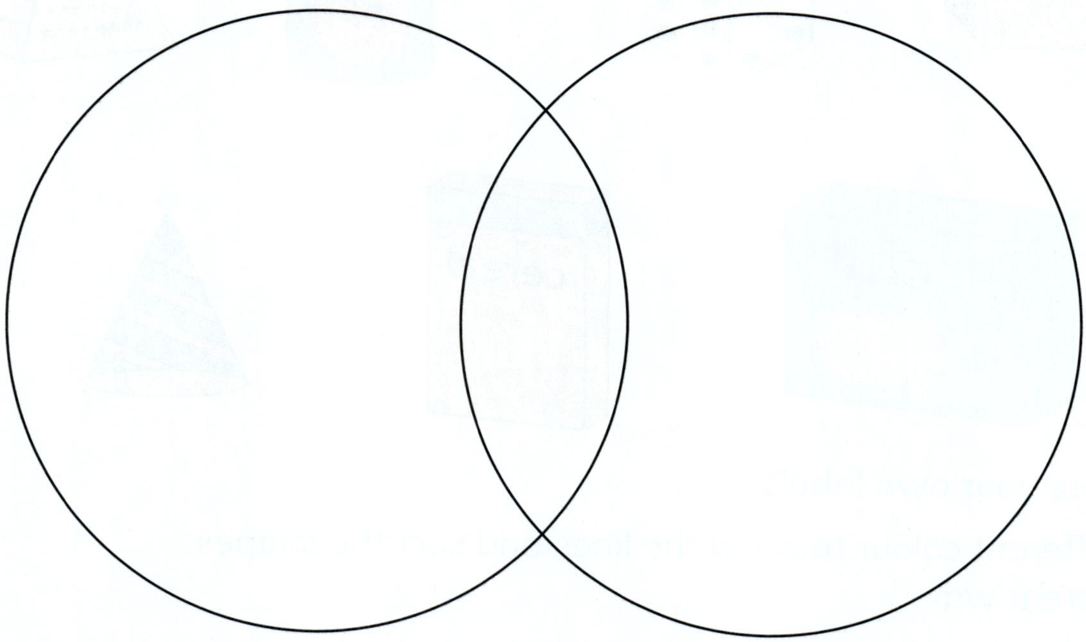

Are there any shapes in the overlap?
What are the names of those shapes?

____

____

3 Choose any three shapes from below.

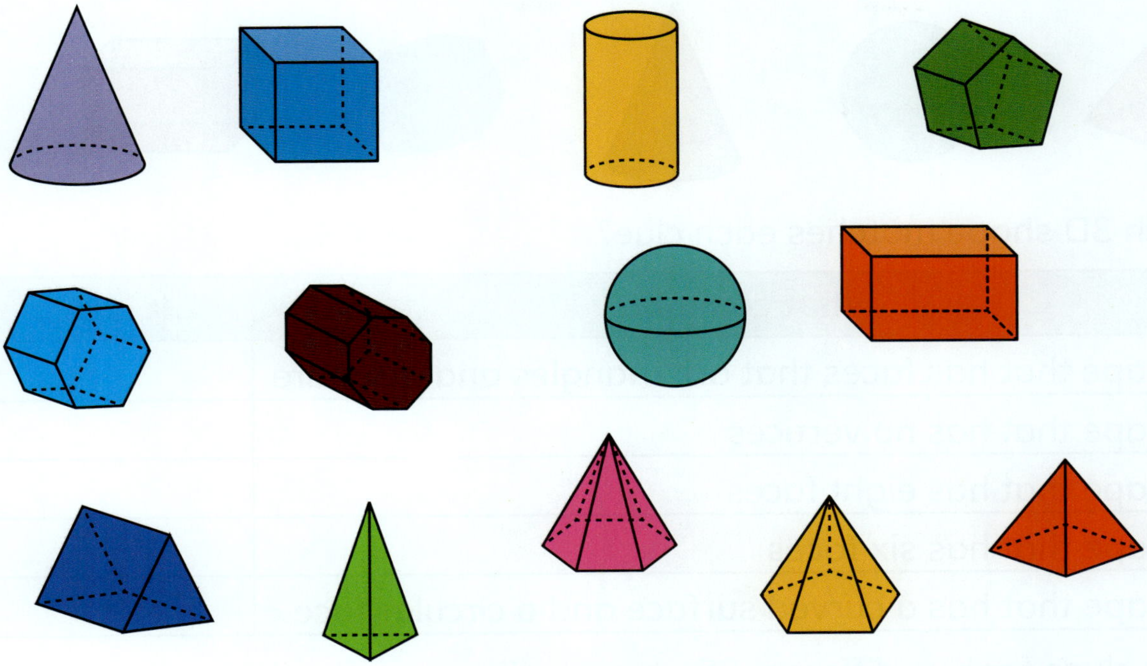

Write what you would say to describe the shapes.

Do not say the name of the shape.

Sketch the shapes you have described.

4 Look at these 3D shapes.

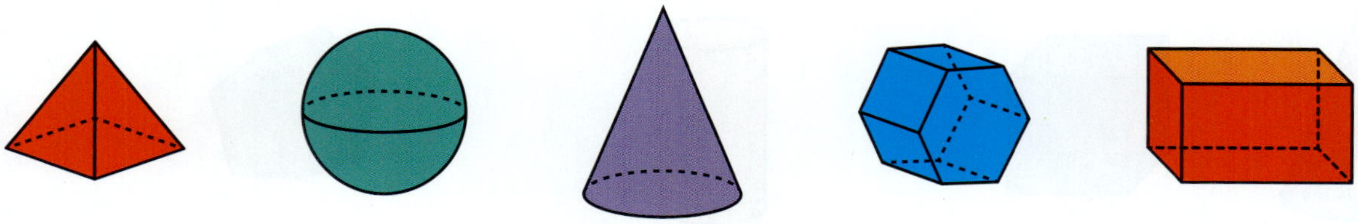

Which 3D shape matches each clue?

What can it be?	It is a ...
A shape that has faces that are triangles and a square	
A shape that has no vertices	
A shape that has eight faces	
A shape that has six faces	
A shape that has a curved surface and a circular face	

Write clues for two different 3D shapes. Give your clue to your partner. Can they identify the shape?

1 ______________________________

2 ______________________________

5 Put a ring around the prisms.

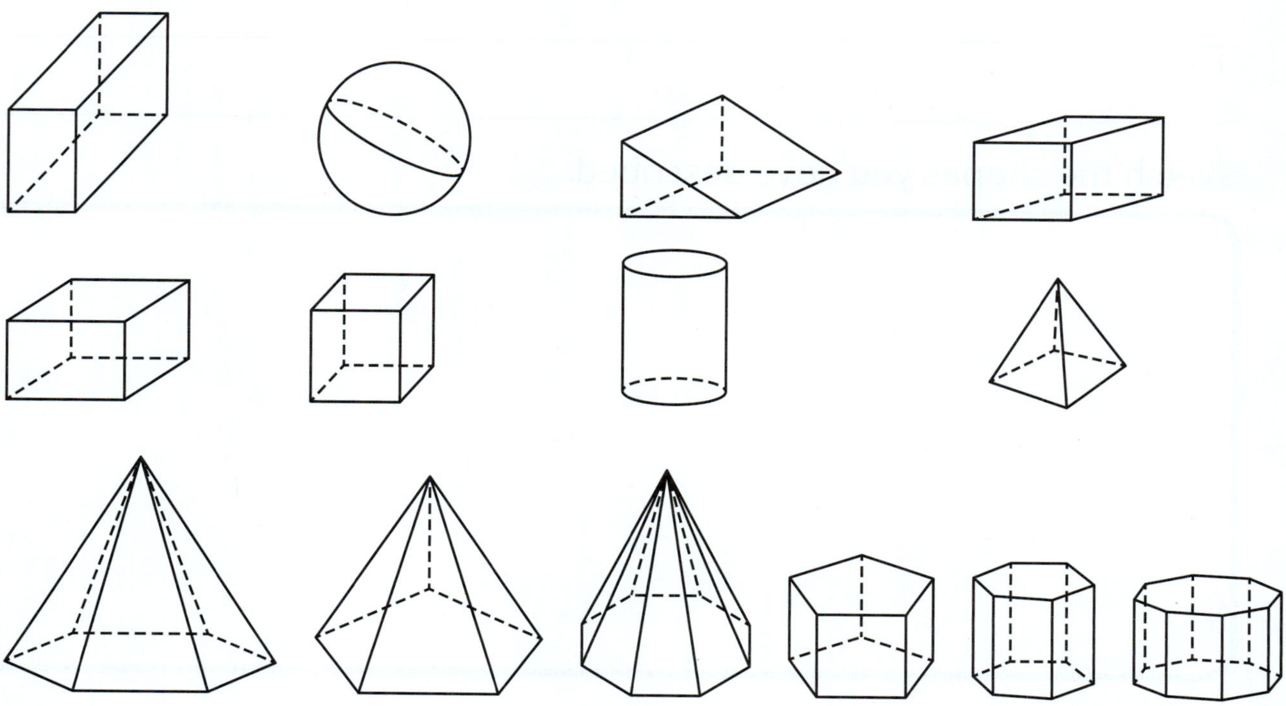

How do you know they are prisms?

____

Why aren't the other shapes prisms?

____

6 Write the name of the shape and say whether it is a prism, a pyramid or neither. Add the properties of each shape.

	Name of shape	Prism, pyramid or neither	Properties
			_____ edges _____ faces _____ vertices
			_____ edges _____ faces _____ vertices
			_____ edges _____ faces _____ vertices
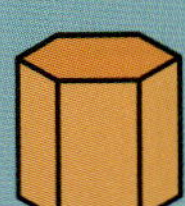			_____ edges _____ faces _____ vertices
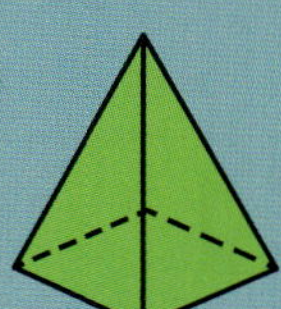			_____ edges _____ faces _____ vertices

Sketch a prism. Sketch a pyramid.

7 You will need a dice and a set of coloured counters in two different colours.

Take turns to roll the dice and look at the key to find a mathematical property.
Place a counter on one of the shapes that has this property.

Each shape can have only one counter on it. Once a counter is there, it cannot be removed.

Keep playing until all the shapes are covered.

The winner is the player with the most counters on the shapes.

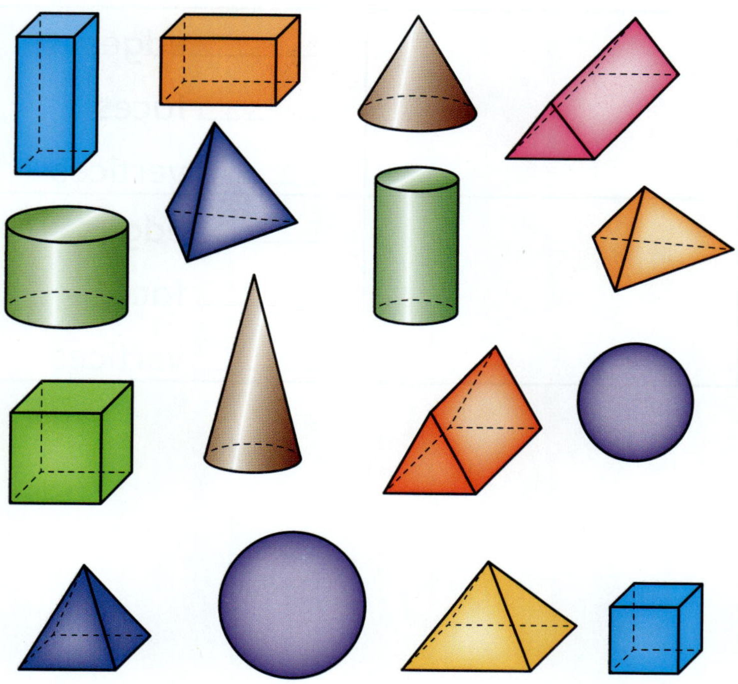

Dice key

 Symmetrical	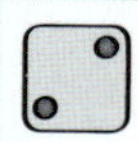 All faces are identical
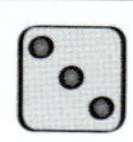 At least one triangular face	 At least one circular face
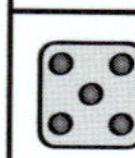 At least one rectangular face	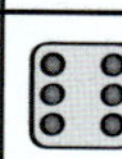 All faces are squares

8 Work with a partner.

Sketch a cuboid.

Sketch two cubes joined together.

Choose another 3D shape to sketch. Name it.

Think like a mathematician

How many cubes would you need to make each of these rectangular prisms?

a

b

c

d

Count the number of cubes used each time.
Can you see a pattern or a rule?

Choose a different number of cubes.
How many different rectangular prisms can you make?

Look for number patterns or rules. What do you notice?

Compare the results of your investigation with a partner's results. If you were going to do the investigation again, would you do something different?

How does working systematically help you make sure that you have found all the possible rectangular prisms?

9 You will need some straws and something to stick the straws together, such as some plasticene or clay.

Here are some shapes made from straws and clay.

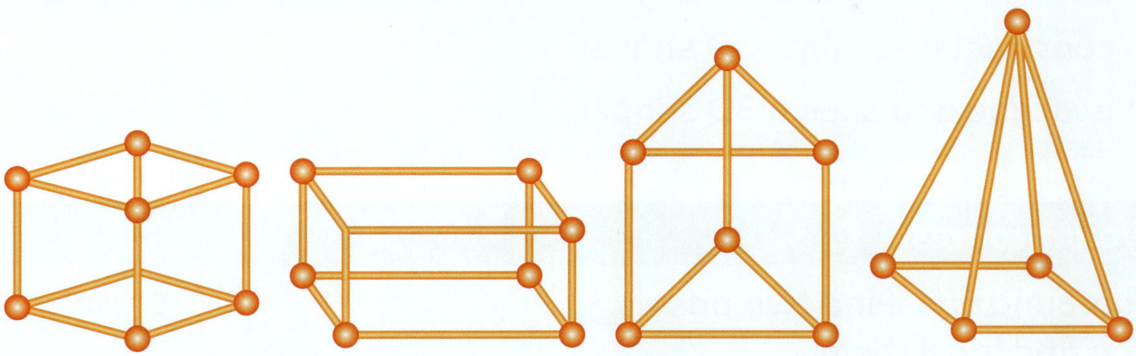

Use your straws to make some other 3D shapes.

For example:

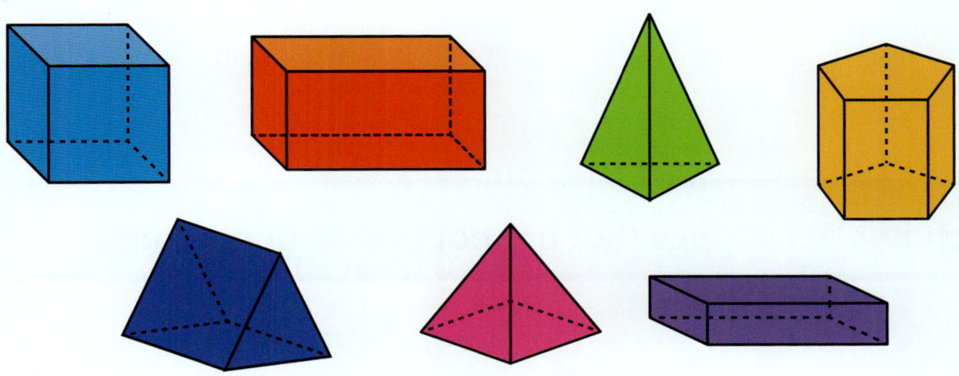

Choose four of the shapes that you have made.

Name them, draw them and list their properties.

Name	Draw	Properties

Look what I can do!

- ☐ I can find what is the same and what is different between prisms and pyramids.
- ☐ I can construct and name 3D shapes.
- ☐ I can describe and sketch 3D shapes.

Check your progress

1 Look around you. Find two prisms.
Sketch and label them.

2 Sketch two 3D shapes that are not prisms or pyramids.

Explain why they are not prisms or pyramids.

____

____

____

3 What is the difference between a prism and a pyramid?

____

____

Project 2

Prism to pyramid

Zara has some straws and some balls of modelling clay that she is using to make 3D shapes.
She starts by creating a triangular prism.

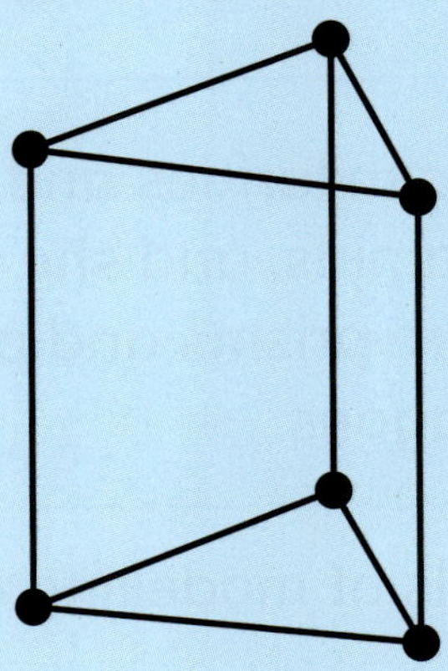

How many straws does she use?
How many balls of modelling clay?

Zara decides to remove some straws and balls of clay to make her shape into a triangular pyramid instead.

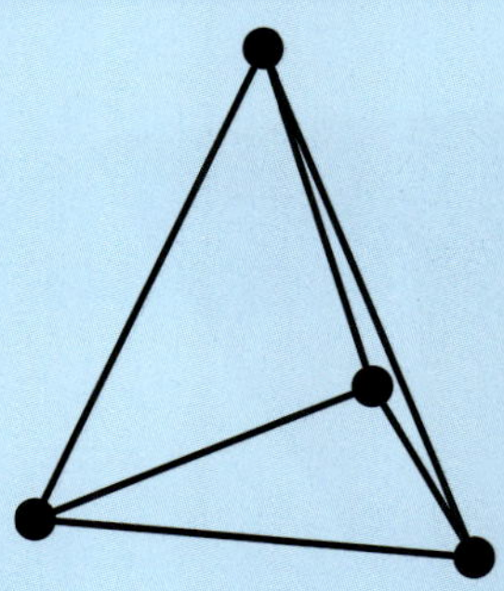

How is this shape similar to the triangular prism?
How is it different? What do you notice about the straws and balls of modelling clay?

Continued

Zara decides to make another prism and turn it into a pyramid, this time with a square base.

How many straws and balls of modelling clay will she need to make the prism? How will she change the shape to turn it into a pyramid?

Zara spots some interesting similarities and differences between the prisms and pyramids, and she decides to investigate further. She makes some more prisms and pyramids with bases that are pentagons and hexagons.

How many straws and balls of modelling clay will Zara use for each shape?

Can you see any interesting similarities and differences between the prisms and pyramids? Can you use this to explain how the number of straws and balls of modelling clay will change each time Zara turns a prism into a pyramid?

5 Multiplication and division

Getting started

1 You know the multiplication tables for 1, 2, 5 and 10.
Write all the multiplication facts with a product of 10.

What do you notice about the multiplication facts that you have written?

2 You also know the matching division facts for the multiplication tables for 1, 2, 5 and 10.
Write all the division facts with a quotient of 5.

3 Arun counted on in tens. Write the next four numbers.

174, 184, 194, ☐, ☐, ☐, ☐

When you have more than one group all the same size, you can multiply together the group size and how many groups, to find out how many all together. You can do this for numbers, people, objects, lengths or prices. You will do this many times in lots of different situations.

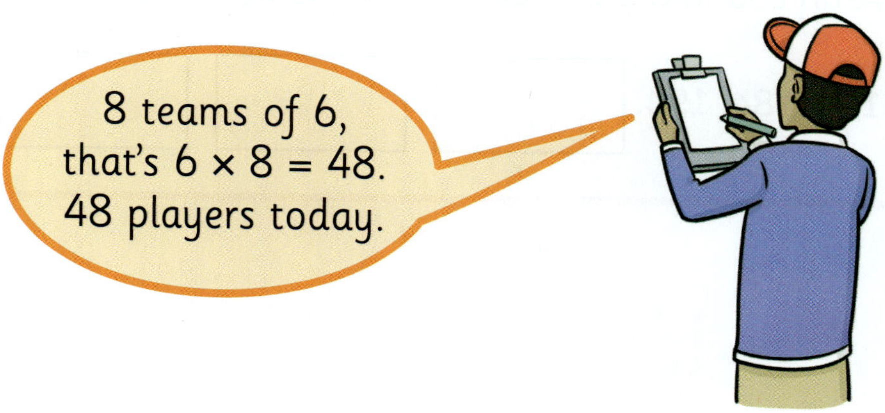

5.1 Exploring multiplication and division

We are going to ...

- recognise multiples of 2, 5 and 10
- make multiplication and division fact families
- multiply single-digit and 2-digit numbers by 10.

Knowing the pattern of the multiples of a number and describing those patterns using words such as odd and even helps you to remember them or work them out. You can connect multiplication and division facts in a fact family just like you did with addition and subtraction.

array commutative
multiple pattern
sequence term
term-to-term rule

Exercise 5.1

1 Draw a ring around all the multiples of 2 in the cloud.

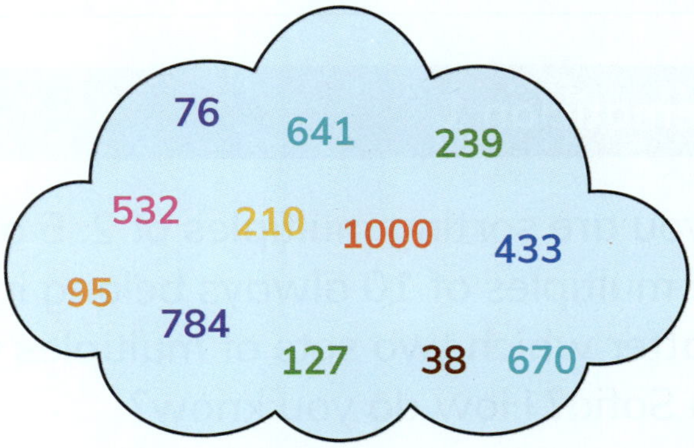

2 Why are multiples of 2 also even numbers?

___

___

3 Sort these numbers into the correct place on the Venn diagram.

45, 120, 132, 401, 740, 215, 805, 490, 96, 387, 350, 675.

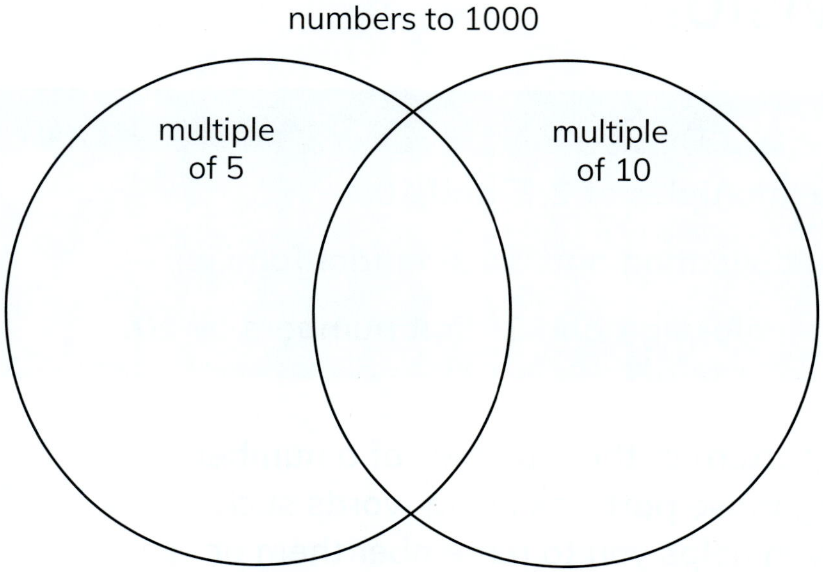

What do you notice about the Venn diagram? Describe the numbers in each part of the Venn diagram, using the words **multiple**, **odd** and **even**.

____

____

____

Think like a mathematician 1

Sofia says that if you are sorting multiples of 2, 5 or 10 in a Venn diagram, the multiples of 10 always belong in the overlap and it does not matter which two sets of multiples you sort.
Do you agree with Sofia? How do you know?

Arun says that multiples of 10 are special numbers.
Why do you think Arun says that?

4 Write the fact family for this array.

☐ × ☐ = ☐	☐ ÷ ☐ = ☐
☐ × ☐ = ☐	☐ ÷ ☐ = ☐
☐ = ☐ × ☐	☐ = ☐ ÷ ☐
☐ = ☐ × ☐	☐ = ☐ ÷ ☐

5 Monifa writes the fact family for 3×10:

$3 \times 10 = 30$, $10 \times 3 = 30$, $30 = 3 \times 10$, $30 = 10 \times 3$,

$30 \div 10 = 3$, $30 = 10 \div 3$, $30 \div 3 = 10$, $30 = 3 \div 10$.

Is Monifa correct? How do you know? Correct any mistakes.

____

____

Think like a mathematician 2

How is finding a fact family for a multiplication fact the same as finding a fact family for an addition fact?

How is it different?

6 Choose three single-digit numbers and three 2-digit numbers to multiply by 10. Record your multiplications.

	× 10 =			× 10 =	
	× 10 =			× 10 =	
	× 10 =			× 10 =	

7 Explain what happens to a single-digit number and a 2-digit number when it is multiplied by 10.
Is the answer always an even number? Why?
You could use the place value chart to help you.

100s	10s	1s

8 A school has 23 boxes of 10 pencils.
How many pencils does the school have? Show your method.

9 The term-to-term rule is: the next term is five more than the previous term. What are the next four numbers in the sequence?

6, 11, ☐, ☐, ☐, ☐

Look what I can do!

- ☐ I can recognise multiples of 2, 5 and 10.
- ☐ I can write the multiplication and division fact families for any facts in the multiplication tables for 1, 2, 5 and 10.
- ☐ I can multiply single-digit and 2-digit numbers by 10.

5.2 Connecting 2 ×, 4 × and 8 ×

We are going to ...

- build the multiplication tables for 4 and 8
- connect the multiplication tables for 2, 4 and 8
- count in fours or eights from any start number.

When you know the multiplication table for 2, you can use it to find other multiplication tables by doubling. You can use the patterns of the multiples to help you count in twos, fours or eights from any number. All the multiples of two are even numbers and multiples of four and eight can be made from multiples of two, so they are even numbers too.

Exercise 5.2

1 Which multiplication from the multiplication table for 4 is represented in the diagram? Remember to count the number of sides on each square.

☐ × ☐ = ☐

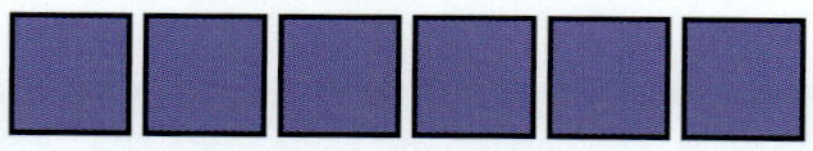

2 What are the next five multiples of 4? Describe the numbers you have written using the words **multiple**, **odd** and **even**.

4, 8, 12, 16, 20, ☐, ☐, ☐, ☐, ☐

Worked example

Write the missing multiplication facts.

2 x 6 = 12	double →	
	← halve	4 x 9 = 36

All multiplications tables facts are group size x how many groups = product.

When you change the group size, you must change the product in the same way.

Double the 2x table fact to find the 4x table fact, because double 2 = 4.

2 x 6 = 12, double → 4 x 6 = 24.

Halve the 4x table fact to find the 2x table fact, because half of 4 = 2.

2 x 9 = 18 ← halve 4 x 9 = 36.

2 x 6 = 12	double →	4 x 6 = 24
2 x 9 = 18	← halve	4 x 9 = 36

3 Write the missing multiplication facts.

$2 \times 7 = 14$	double →	
	double →	$4 \times 3 = 12$
$2 \times 5 = 10$	← halve	
	← halve	$4 \times 4 = 16$

4 Which multiplication fact is represented in the diagram?

☐ × ☐ = ☐

Tip

Count the number of legs on each spider.

5 Colour all the multiples of 8.

71	72	73	74	75	76	77	78	79	80
81	82	83	84	85	86	87	88	89	90
91	92	93	94	95	96	97	98	99	100
101	102	103	104	105	106	107	108	109	110
111	112	113	114	115	116	117	118	119	120

Describe the numbers you have coloured using the words **multiple, odd** and **even.**

___

6 Write the missing multiplication facts.

$2 \times 9 = 18$	double →		double →	
	double →		double →	$8 \times 5 = 40$
	← halve	$4 \times 6 = 24$	← halve	
$2 \times 3 = 6$	← halve		← halve	

Tip

Remember to change the group size and the product in the same way to find the new multiplication table fact. The number of groups does not change.

If you sorted the multiples of 4 and the multiples of 8 on to a Venn diagram, which part of the diagram would be empty? Why?

7 The term-to-term rule is add 4.

Start at 5. What are the next five numbers in the sequence?

5, ☐, ☐, ☐, ☐, ☐.

Describe the numbers you have written using the words **multiple**, **odd** and **even**.

____

8 What is the term-to-term rule in this sequence?
What are the missing numbers?

3, 11, 19, ☐, 35, ☐

Describe the numbers you have written using the words **multiple**, **odd** and **even**.

___

The term-to-term rule is ______________.

9 Two of the five numbers in Jamal's sequence are 13 and 29.
What could the other numbers in his sequence be?
What could his term-to-term rule be?

Find another solution.

Think like a mathematician

Zara conjectures that if the term-to-term rule is an even number, then the terms will all be even if the start number is even.

Is Zara's conjecture correct? How do you know?

Share your investigation with a friend. Do you agree?

Look what I can do!

- ☐ I can work out and use the multiplication tables for 4 and 8.
- ☐ I can connect the multiplication tables for 2, 4 and 8 by doubling.
- ☐ I can count in fours or eights from any start number.

5.3 Connecting 3 ×, 6 × and 9 ×

We are going to ...

- build the multiplication tables for 3, 6 and 9
- connect the multiplication tables for 3, 6 and 9
- count in threes, sixes or nines from any start number.

When you know one multiplication table, you can use it to find other multiplication tables by doubling, adding or subtracting. You can use the patterns of the multiples to help you count on or count back from any number. Describing the patterns of the numbers using words such as odd and even helps you to notice and correct any mistakes.

counting stick

Exercise 5.3

1 Write the multiples of 3 and 6.

	1	2	3	4	5	6	7	8	9	10
3 ×	3				15					
6 ×	6									60

2 Which multiplication facts from the multiplication tables for 3 and 6 have the same value? The first one is done for you.

3 × 2 = 6 × 1

3 Write the missing multiplication facts.

	double →	6 × 5 = 30
3 × 7 = 21	double →	
	← halve	6 × 8 = 48
3 × 9 = 27	← halve	

Tip

Remember to change the group size and the product in the same way to find the new multiplication table fact.

4 Colour the multiples of 9 on this 100 square. Describe the pattern you make.

1	2	3	4	5	6	7	8	9	10
11	12	13	14	15	16	17	18	19	20
21	22	23	24	25	26	27	28	29	30
31	32	33	34	35	36	37	38	39	40
41	42	43	44	45	46	47	48	49	50
51	52	53	54	55	56	57	58	59	60
61	62	63	64	65	66	67	68	69	70
71	72	73	74	75	76	77	78	79	80
81	82	83	84	85	86	87	88	89	90
91	92	93	94	95	96	97	98	99	100

5 Doubling the multiplication table for 6 does not give the multiplication table for 9. What could you do instead? Give an example.

6 Multiply the numbers in the bricks next to each other to find the number for the brick above.

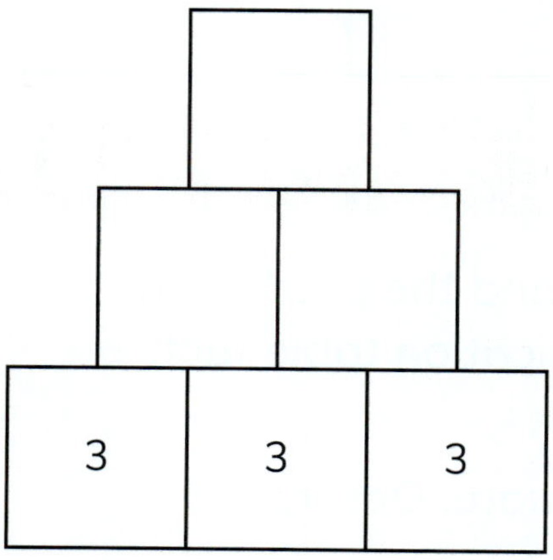

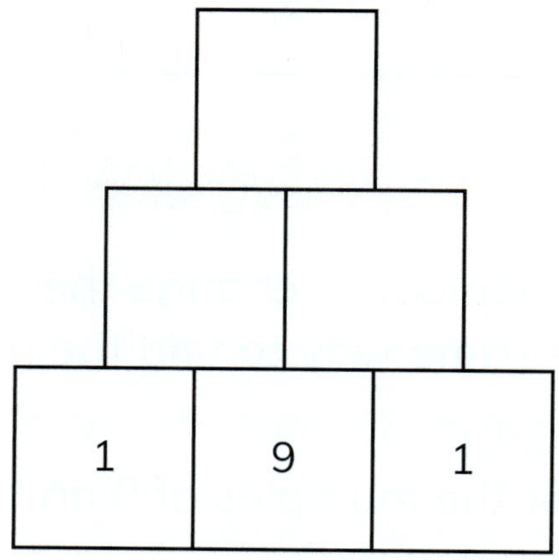

Where have you seen walls like this before? What were they used for?

7 a The term-to-term rule is add 9. Choose a start number and write the first five numbers in your sequence.

☐, ☐, ☐, ☐, ☐.

b When the start number is the same as the term-to-term rule, how can you describe the numbers in the sequence? For example, start at 9, term-to-term rule is add 9.

8 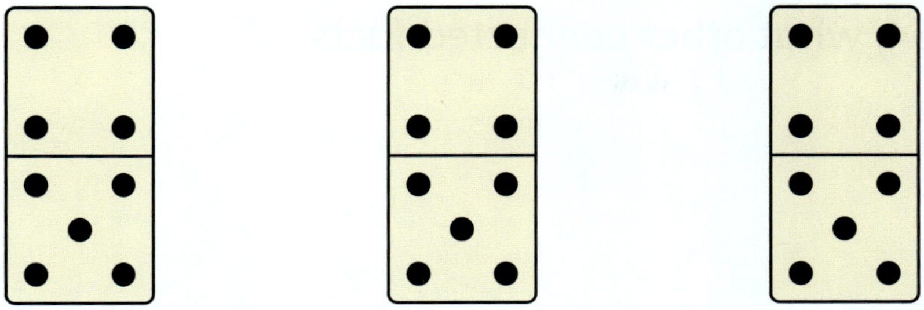

$9 \times 3 = \underbrace{5 \times 3} + \underbrace{4 \times 3} = 15 + 12 = 27$

Draw a picture to show how you can add the multiplication tables for 5 and 3 together to find 8 × 4.

Compare your drawing with that of a friend.
How are your drawings the same?
How are they different?

9 If you know that $6 \times 9 = 54$, what other connected facts do you know?

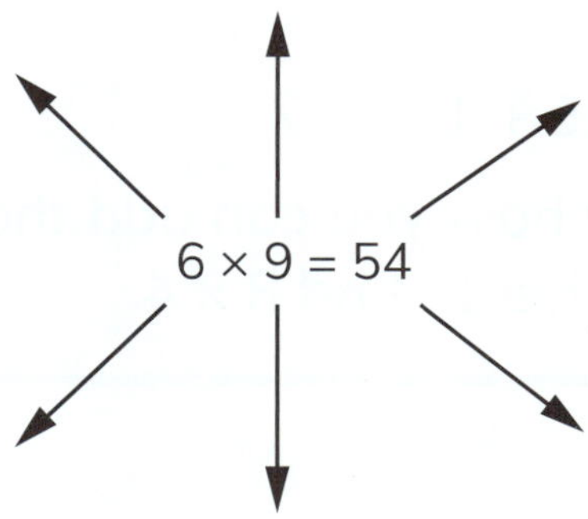

Think like a mathematician

The digit sum of a number is found by adding the digits together; for example, the digit sum of 24 is $2 + 4 = 6$.
If the sum is more than 9, repeat until you have a single digit; for example, the digit sum of 48 is $4 + 8 = 12$, $1 + 2 = 3$.

Is there a pattern in the digit sums of the multiples of 3, 6 and 9?

Look what I can do!

- ☐ I can build the multiplication tables for 3, 6 and 9.
- ☐ I can connect the multiplication tables for 3, 6 and 9 through doubling and adding.
- ☐ I can count in threes, sixes or nines from any start number.

Check your progress

1 Write the multiplication and division fact family for this array.

Continued

2 Draw a ring around the numbers that are multiples of 2, 5 <u>and</u> 10.

32 50 125 288 340 95

580 456 924 700 10

3 Complete each multiplication fact.

$8 \times 10 =$ $10 \times 3 =$ $27 \times 10 =$

$9 \times 5 =$ $4 \times 8 =$ $6 \times 7 =$

$5 \times 4 =$ $8 \times 6 =$ $3 \times 9 =$

4 The term-to-term rule is + 6.

Start at 7. What are the next five numbers in the sequence?

7, , , , , .

6 Measurement, area and perimeter

Getting started

1 Use a ruler and a pencil to draw lines of these lengths on a piece of paper:

a 2 centimetres

b 8 centimetres

c between 5 and 6 centimetres

d more than 3 centimetres but less than 14 centimetres.

2 Estimate and measure the length of:

a your hand ____________

b your shoe ____________

c a pencil ____________

d a book ____________

In this unit you will be learning more about measurement.

Kilometres are units used to measure long distances.

Perimeter is the distance around a space.

Area is the space inside the perimeter.

6.1 Measurement

We are going to ...

- estimate and measure lengths in centimetres, metres and kilometres, rounding to the nearest whole number
- understand the relationships between the units of length.

This section will use measurements of length, including kilometres.

You will use estimation and rounding when you measure.

You will work with both regular and irregular shapes.

centimetre (cm)
kilometre (km)
metre (m)
rounding

Worked example 1

Estimate and then measure the length of this line.

estimate = ________ measure = ________

How close was your estimate?

estimate = 10 cm

measure = 11 cm

My estimate was quite close.

When you are estimating, you do not need to be exact. When you are measuring, the measurement needs to be exact.

Exercise 6.1

1 Find a way to measure the length of your step.

With a partner choose a long distance to measure.

Measure the distance in steps. The ____________ is ☐ steps long.

Measure the length again using a metre stick.

How many metres long is it?

The ____________ is ☐ metres long.

Are the number of steps and the number of metres the same? Explain why/why not.

____

____

2 Look around your classroom to find objects that are between $\frac{1}{2}$ metre and 1 metre long.
Estimate the length of each object. Record the estimate.

Measure each object to the nearest centimetre.
Record the actual length.

Object	Estimated length	Actual length

3 What would you use to measure these?
Draw your answers in the table below.

Item	I would use ...
Distance between two continents	
Length of a seal	
Size of a saucepan	
An Olympic marathon	
Length of your foot	

Item	I would use ...
Length of a rowing boat	
Width of a mobile phone	
Length of a golf course	
Height of your bedroom door	
Width of a glove	

4 Use a ruler.
Draw a square with sides of 6 cm.

Draw two more squares and two rectangles using different measurements.

Write the measurements along the sides.

5 On centimetre squared paper draw four different rectangles with a perimeter of 24 cm.

Estimate the area of each.

Count the squares to work out the area of each rectangle.

Record what you find out.

Length	Width	Perimeter	Estimated area (square units)	Actual area (square units)

On centimetre squared paper, draw four different rectangles with an area of 20 square cm.

Complete this table.

Length	Width	Perimeter (cm)	Area (square units)
			20
			20
			20
			20

6 Use a ruler to measure the length of these objects. Round up or down to the nearest centimetre.

Your finger ______________

Your pencil ______________

A book ______________

Your shoe ______________

Choose four more object to measure. Round the length up or down to the nearest cm.

Record your results.

1 ______________

2 ______________

3 ______________

4 ______________

7 a Draw two lines to make this into a square. Estimate and then measure the length of one side.

estimate = __________

measure = __________

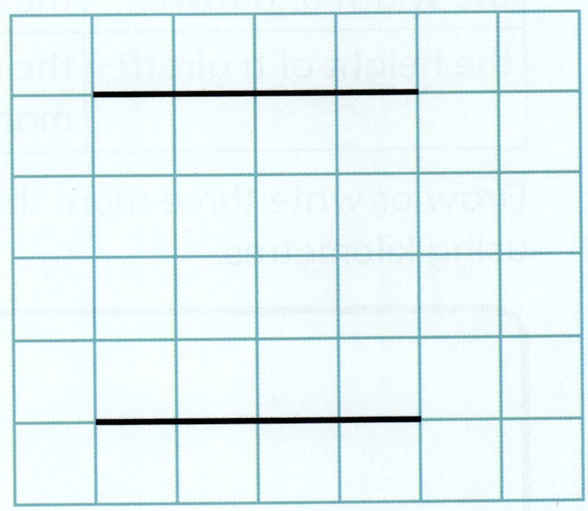

b Draw three lines to make this into a square.

Estimate and then measure the length of one side.

estimate = __________

measure = __________

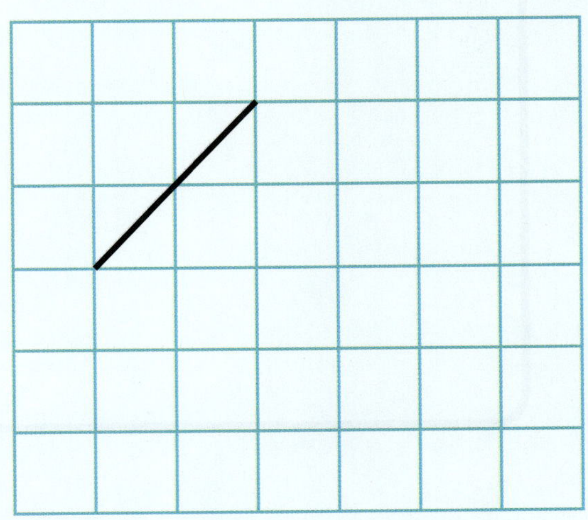

8 Use the tip to help you work out these conversions.

Tip

100 cm = 1 metre

1000 m = 1 kilometre

a 7 m = ______ cm

b 250 cm = ______ m

c 3 and a half metres = ______ cm

d $\frac{1}{2}$ km = ______ m

e 750 m = ______ km

f $\frac{1}{4}$ km = ______ m

9 Circle the things that would be measured using kilometres.

the distance between two continents	the height of a door	the length of a football pitch
the width of a towel	the length of a train	the length of a whale
the height of a giraffe	the distance of a marathon race	the length of a long journey

Draw or write three more things that would be measured using kilometres.

10 Round the measurements of the length of the table, the length of the bed, the length measured by the tape and the distance.

Object	Measurement	Rounded measurement
	length 108 cm	How long is the coffee table? a To the nearest 10 cm? ________________ b To the nearest 100 cm? ________________ ________________
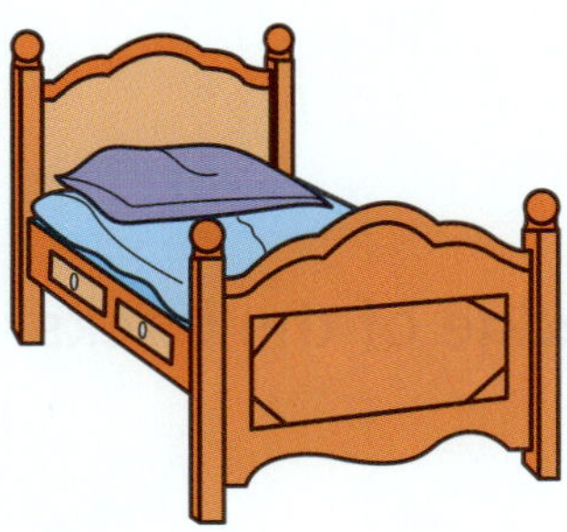	length 275 cm	How long is the bed? a To the nearest 10 cm? ________________ b To the nearest metre? ________________ ________________
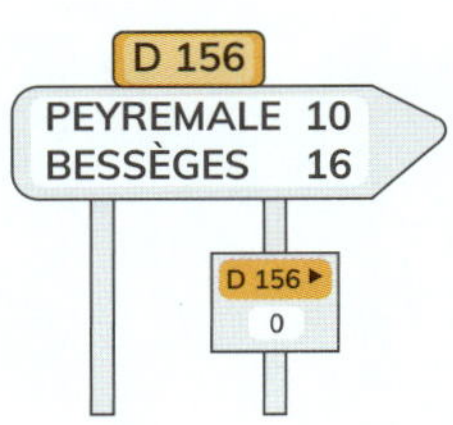	a distance of 16 km	a Round up to the nearest 10 km. ________________ b Round down to the nearest 5 km. ________________ ________________

Think like a mathematician

Silas and Simon are snails. They live on a wall.
They can travel only along the edge of the bricks.
Each brick is 30 cm long and 15 cm wide.

Silas wants to visit Simon.
First, calculate the shortest route, keeping to the edge of the bricks.

Next, calculate two other routes.

Record what you have discovered.

Compare your answers with your partner's answers. Were they the same? Did you both have the same shortest route?

What if the length of the sides of some of the bricks changed? How would that change the shortest route?

Look what I can do!

- [ ] I can estimate and measure lengths in centimetres, metres and kilometres, rounding to the nearest whole number.
- [ ] I can understand the relationships between the units of length.

6.2 2D shapes and perimeter

We are going to ...

- measure perimeter by adding lengths
- draw lines, rectangles and squares and calculate the perimeter of a shape
- find the difference between regular and irregular shapes.

In Stage 2 you learned about regular polygons.

A regular polygon is a shape that has all sides and angles the same size.

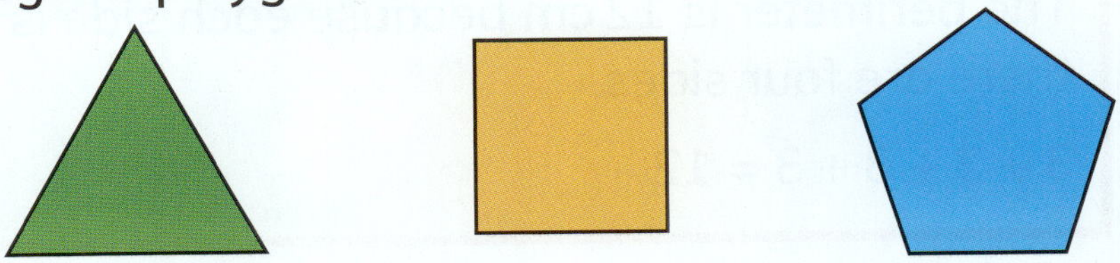

centi irregular shape
kilo perimeter
polygon regular shape

An irregular polygon is a shape that has sides and angles of different sizes.

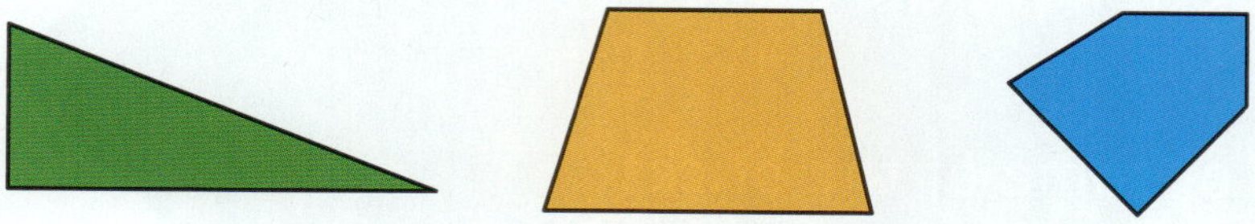

The perimeter of a shape is the total length of all of its sides.

How could you find the perimeter of a shape?

Worked example 2

The perimeter of a shape is the distance around its edge.

Shape A is a square and is drawn on centimetre squared paper.

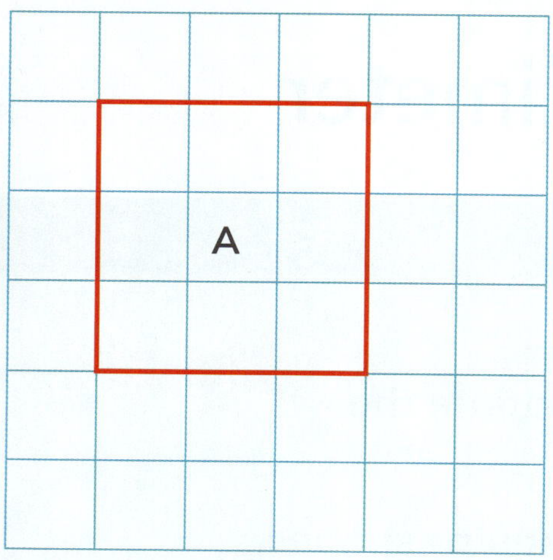

Is its perimeter 9 cm? Explain your answer.

The perimeter is 12 cm because each *side* is 3 cm and there are four sides.

$3 + 3 + 3 + 3 = 12$

Exercise 6.2

1 Complete the sentences to describe these shapes in three different ways.

These shapes all have ______________________________

These shapes all have ______________________________

These shapes all have ______________________________

Sketch two more shapes that have the same properties.

2 Draw a triangle.

Describe your triangle to your partner.

What information do you need to include in your description?

Can they sketch an exact copy of it?

3 These squares are drawn on centimetre squared paper. Explain what happens to the perimeter when the squares get bigger.

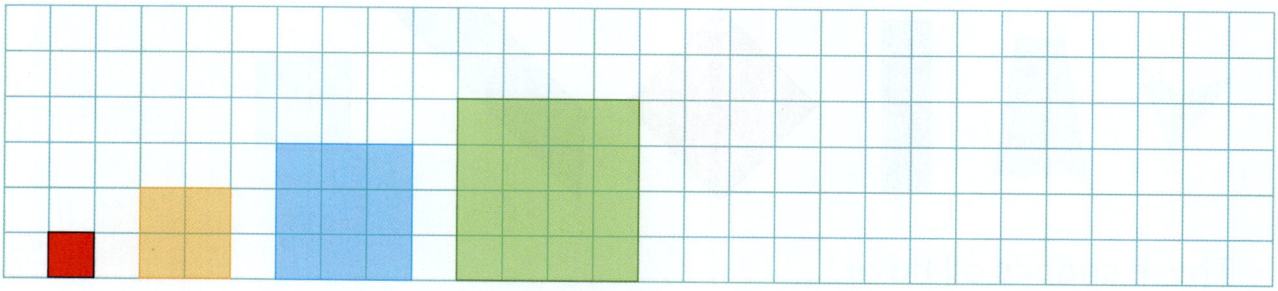

____

____

Draw the next two squares in the sequence and write their perimeters.

4 a Colour the regular shapes.

b Draw a ring around the irregular shapes.

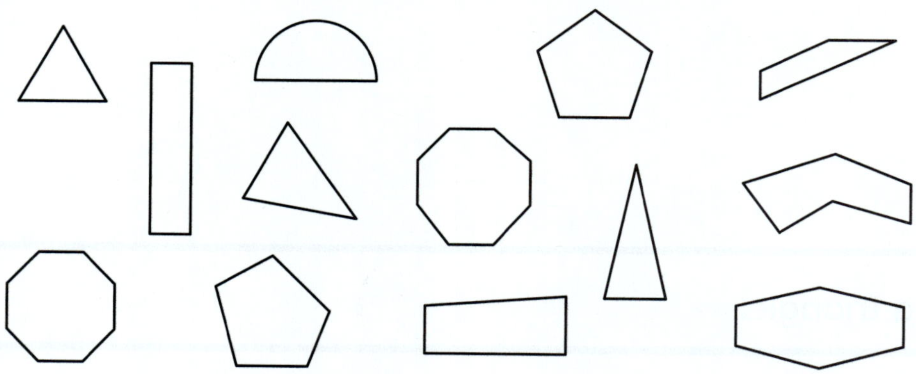

c Draw two regular and two irregular shapes of your own. Label them.

5 Use ten sticks of equal length to make two different shapes that each have a perimeter of 10 units. Draw what you did.

Try with 12 sticks of equal length. Draw what you did.

6 Work out the perimeters of these shapes.

a

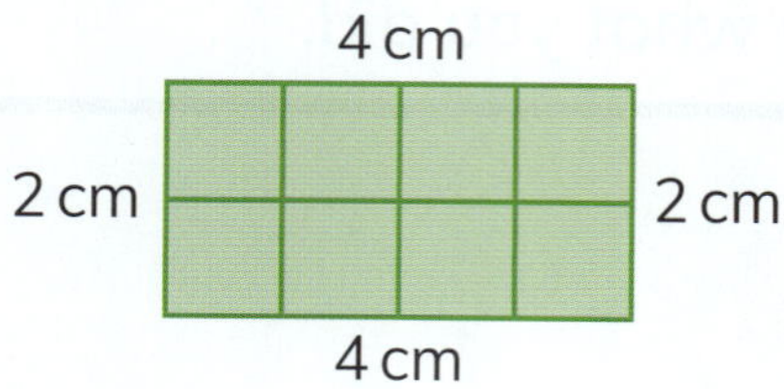

perimeter = ________

b

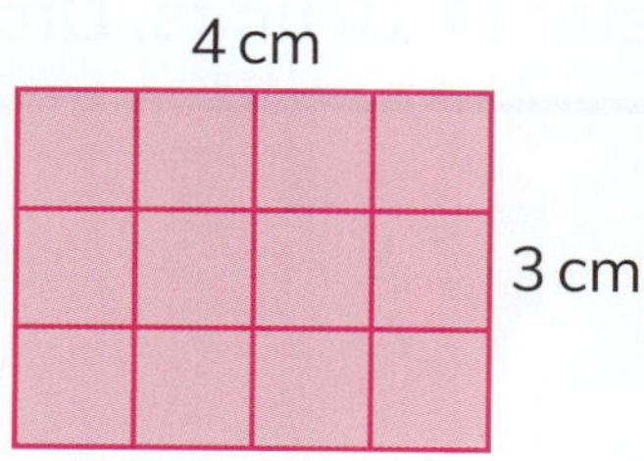

perimeter = ________

c

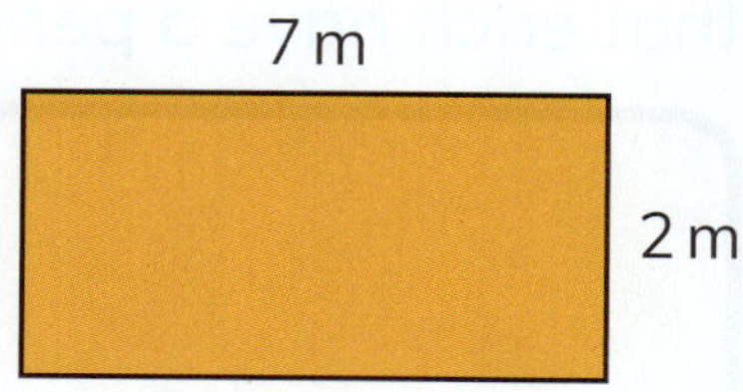

perimeter = ________

d

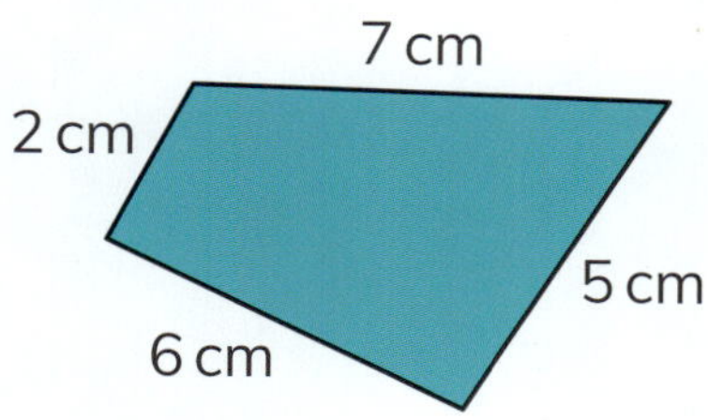

perimeter = ________

e

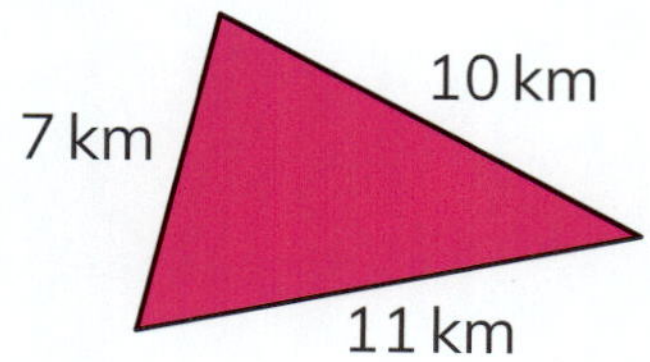

perimeter = ________

f

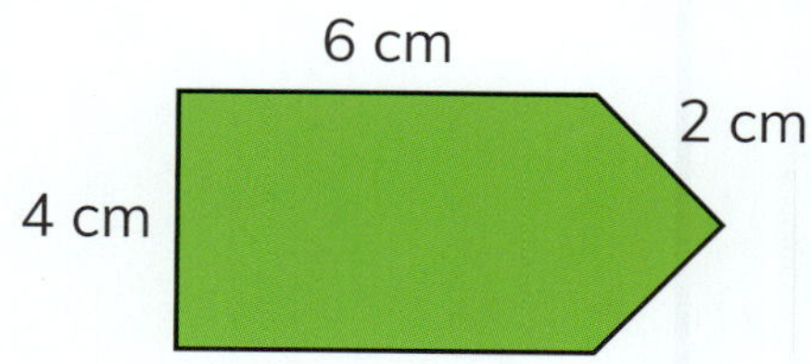

perimeter = ________

Draw your own irregular shape with a perimeter of 23 cm.
How many lines will you use?

Think like a mathematician

This square has sides measuring 6 cm.

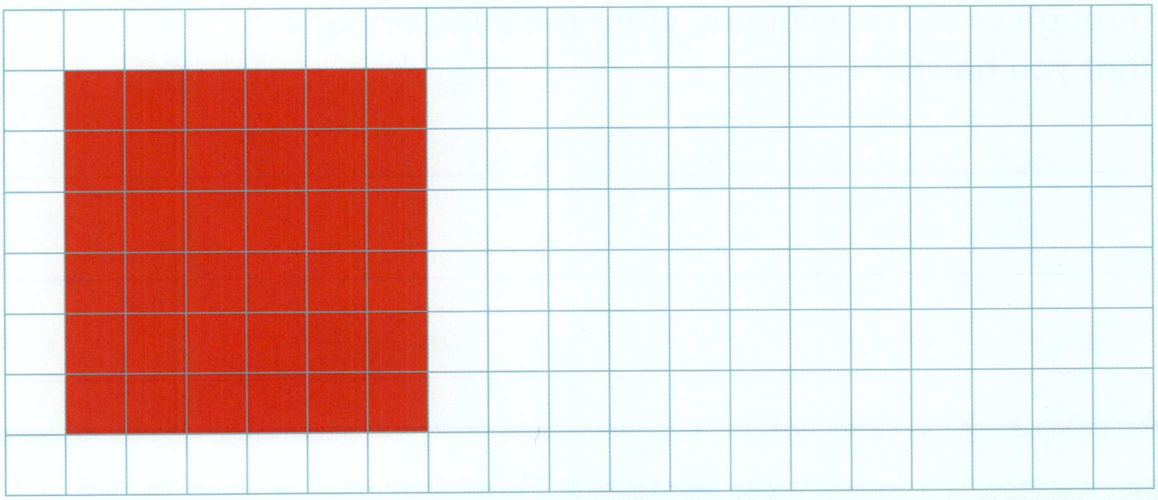

a What is its perimeter?

____

b Taking one row and one column away each time, draw the next two squares. Write their perimeters. ________________

c Imagine and then draw all the remaining squares after that, taking one row and one column each time, until you get to one square.

d For the 6 cm by 6 cm square through to the 1 cm by 1 cm square, write the perimeter of each square.

Continued

e Using all the perimeter values from the 6 cm by 6 cm square through to the one square, write the number pattern that you have.

____

____

____

Compare your answers with your partner's answers. Were they the same? How could you convince your partner that you are right?

What would happen to the perimeter if you used other regular shapes?

Look what I can do!

- ☐ I can measure perimeter by adding lengths.
- ☐ I can draw lines, rectangles and squares and calculate the perimeter of a shape.
- ☐ I know the difference between regular and irregular shapes.

6.3 Introducing area

We are going to ...

- draw lines, rectangles and squares
- estimate, measure and calculate perimeters and areas.

In this section you will learn about area.
Area is the amount of space that a shape covers.

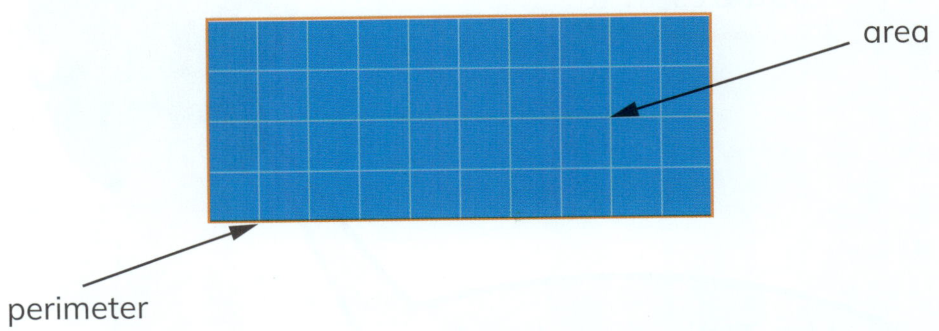

area

square units

You will also do more work on perimeters and find the differences between area and perimeter.

This section uses regular and irregular shapes.

Worked example 3

Sofia and Zara are talking about area.

Who is right?

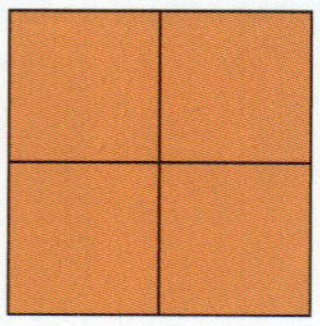

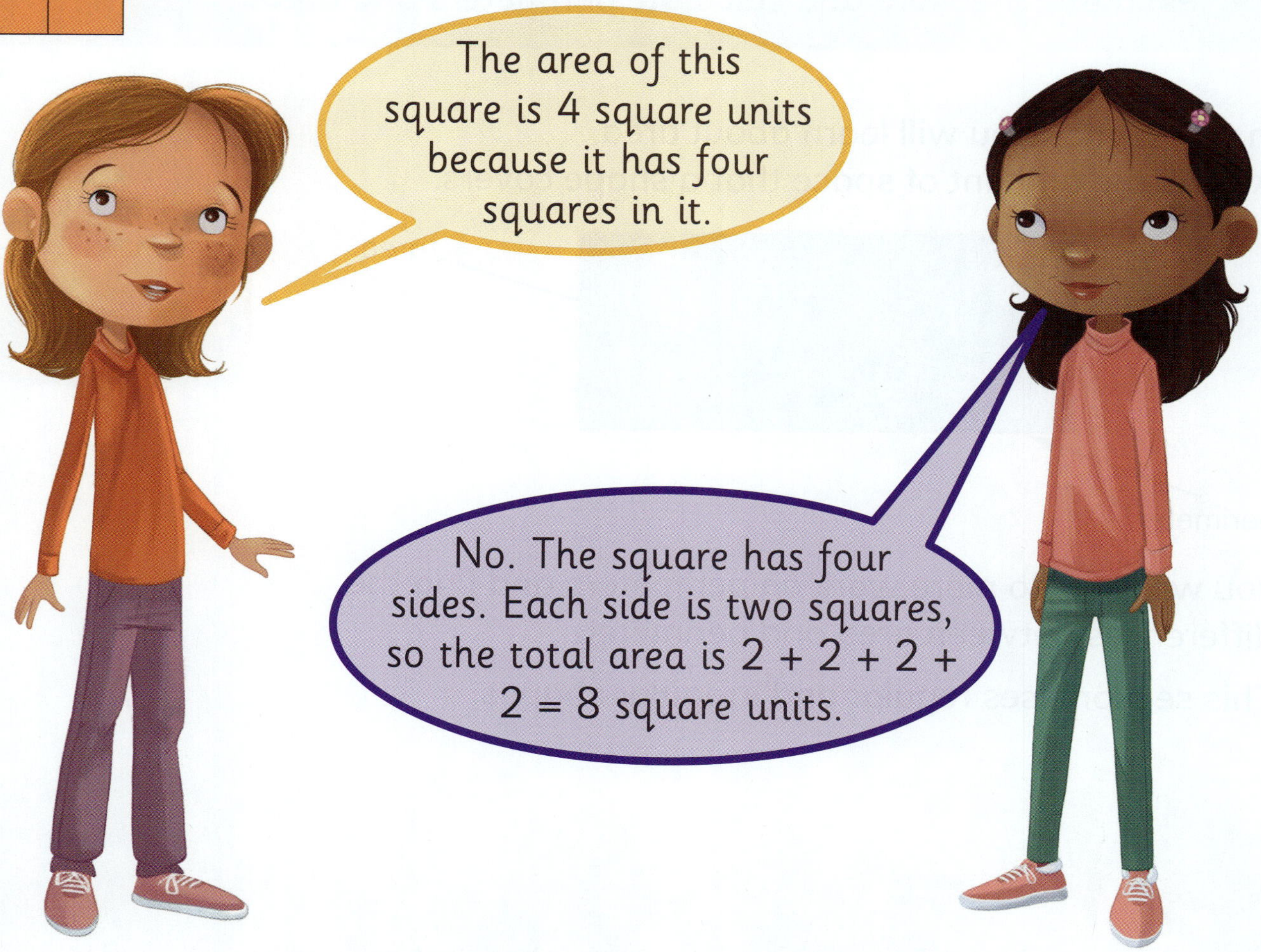

Sofia is right. The area is how much space a shape uses.

This square covers four squares, so the area is 4 square units.

Zara is incorrect because she is counting outside the square.

Exercise 6.3

1 Estimate, measure and calculate the area of these shapes.

Write the estimate below the shape and the area on the shape.

a
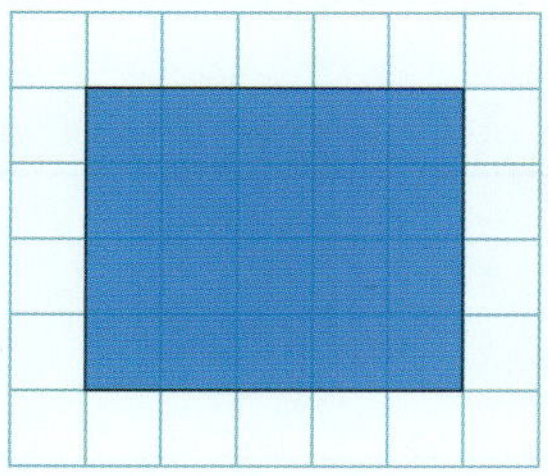

b
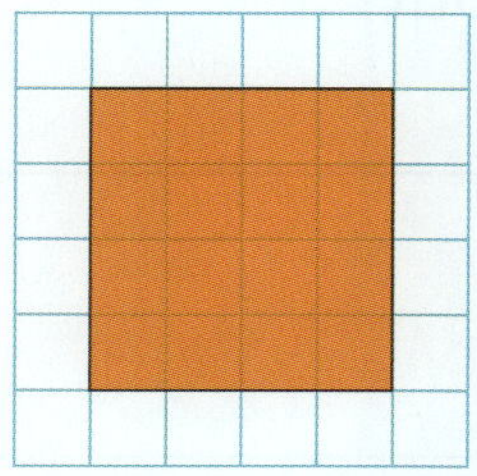

c
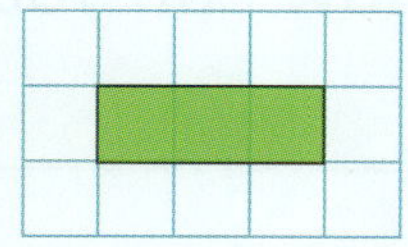

d
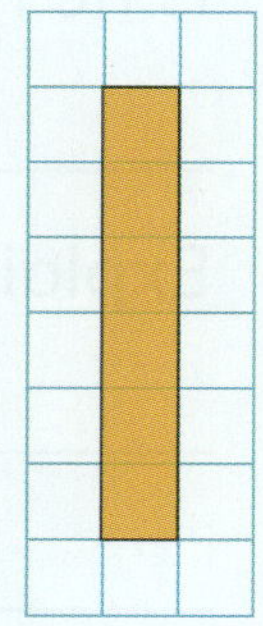

estimate: ______ estimate: ______ estimate: ______ estimate: ______

2 Do you think that these shapes have the same area? Check and find out.

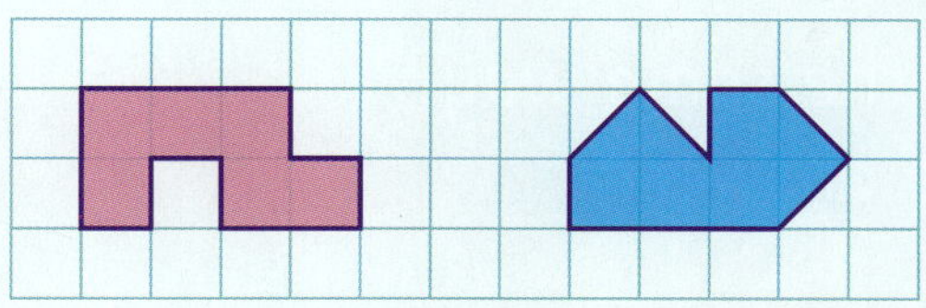

____

____

Make some more shapes that have the same area but look different. Record them on squared paper.

3 a If the area of a square is 81 square units, how long are the sides?

b What is the perimeter? Show how you know.

Think like a mathematician

Thandiwe says, 'All rectangles with a perimeter of 26 metres will have the same area.'

a Is he right? How can you find out?

____

b Explain how you know.

____

____

With a partner, share what you did and what you found out.

Did you both work in the same way?
Did you find the same answer?

Could there be a better or quicker way to find the answer?

Look what I can do!

- [ ] I can draw lines, rectangles and squares.
- [ ] I can estimate, measure and calculate the perimeters and areas.

Check your progress

1 a Round these to the nearest metre or half metre, whichever is closest.

247 cm   724 cm   923 cm

b Round these to the nearest half, quarter or three-quarters of a kilometre, whichever is closest.

527 m   328 m   473 m   803 m

2 Measure the lengths of each of these lines.

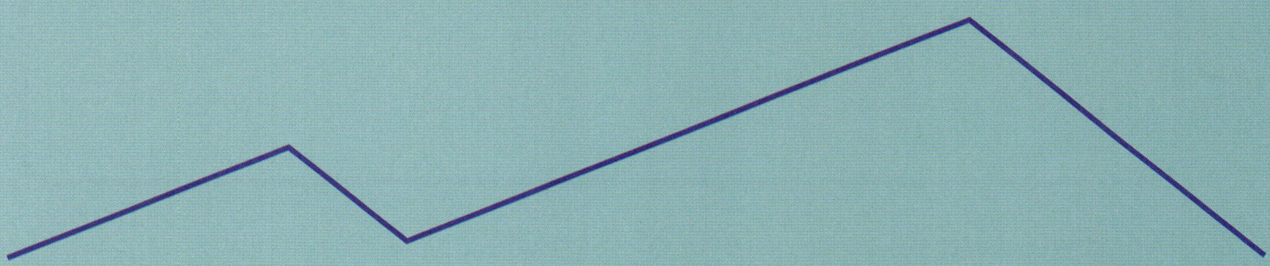

a Calculate the total length.

total: ___________

b Find two ways of making a length 16 cm.

Continued

3 a What are the perimeters of these shapes?

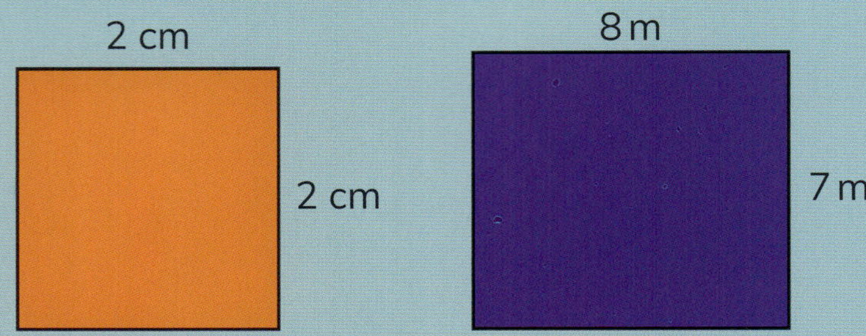

b On a separate piece of squared paper, draw a shape that has a perimeter of 35 cm.

4 a Calculate two possible areas of a shape that has a perimeter of 60 cm.

b Calculate two possible areas of a shape that has a perimeter of 24 units.

c Calculate two possible areas of a shape that has a perimeter of 10 units.

Project 3

Chalky shapes

At Butterfly School, there is a grid painted onto the playground with 1 metre between the lines. Three shapes are drawn on the playground using chalk.

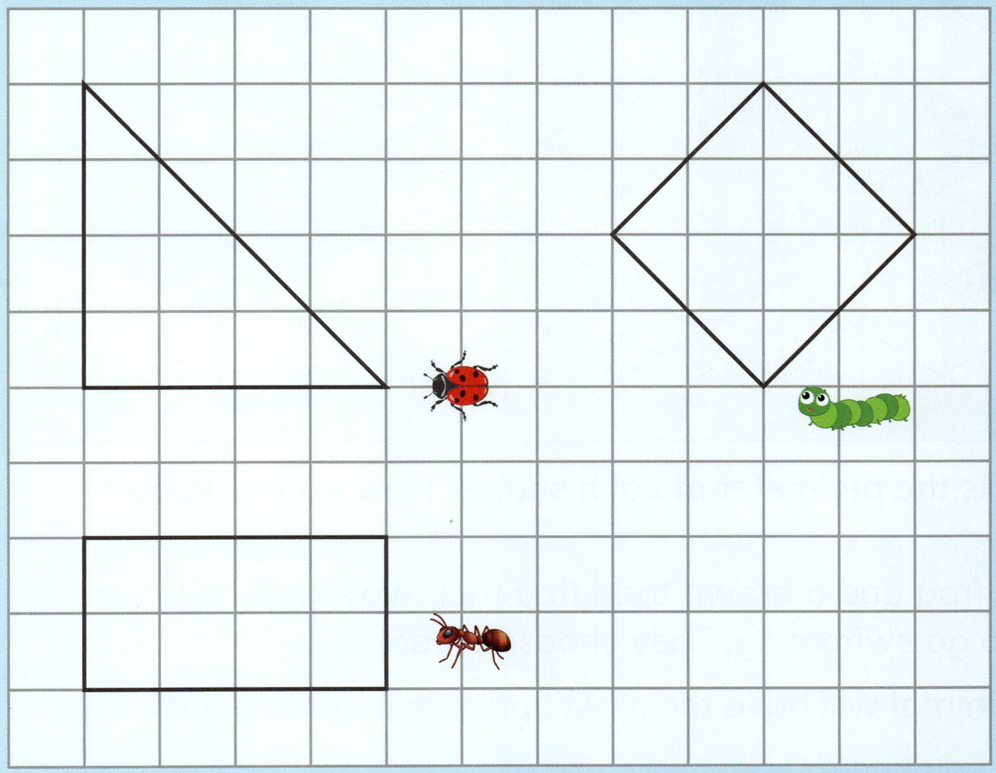

What is the area of each shape? How do you know?

A ladybird, a caterpillar and an ant each choose a shape to walk all the way round and get back to where they started.

Which of these creatures has to walk the longest distance around its shape?

Which of these creatures has to walk the shortest distance around its shape?

How do you know?

Continued

The leisure centre next door to Butterfly School has triangular tiles on the floor. The side of each tile is 1 metre. There are two swimming pools with orange paths around them.

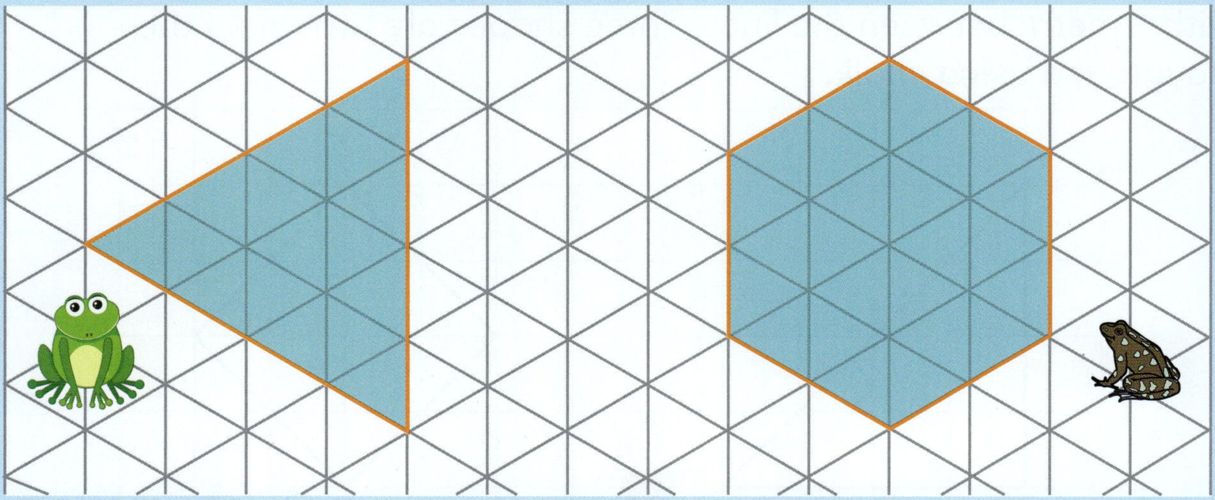

What is the perimeter of each shape? How do you know?

A green frog and a brown toad find their way into the leisure centre to go swimming. They choose a pool to swim in.

Which animal will have the most space to swim around in?

How do you know?

7 Fractions of shapes

Getting started

1 Draw lines to divide these shapes into equal parts according to their labels.

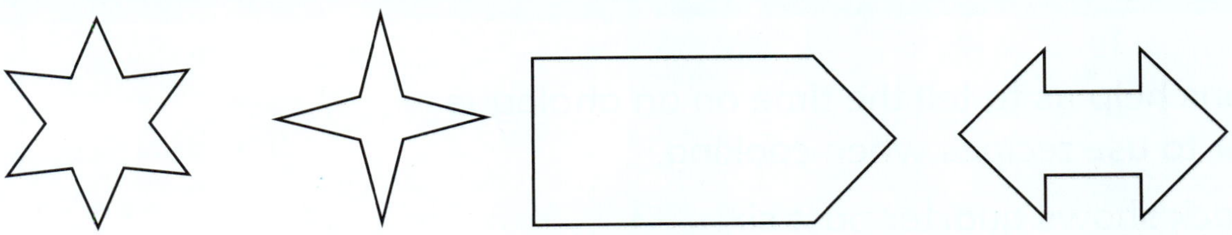

$\frac{1}{4}$ $\frac{1}{4}$ $\frac{1}{2}$ $\frac{1}{2}$

This unit introduces thirds, fifths and tenths.

You will be exploring equal parts of a whole.

You will be finding fractions that can be put together to find new fractions.

> 7.1 Fractions and equivalence of shapes

We are going to ...

- explore thirds, fifths and tenths
- show that two fractions can have equivalent values
- explore the links between the whole and the parts.

denominator
equal equivalent
fifths numerator
tenths thirds

Fractions help us to tell the time on an analogue clock or to use recipes when cooking.

This clock shows quarter past six. What does the quarter relate to?

Worked example 1

For the circle, colour one part red. Colour two parts blue. Colour the rest of the circle green.

What fraction of the circle is each colour?

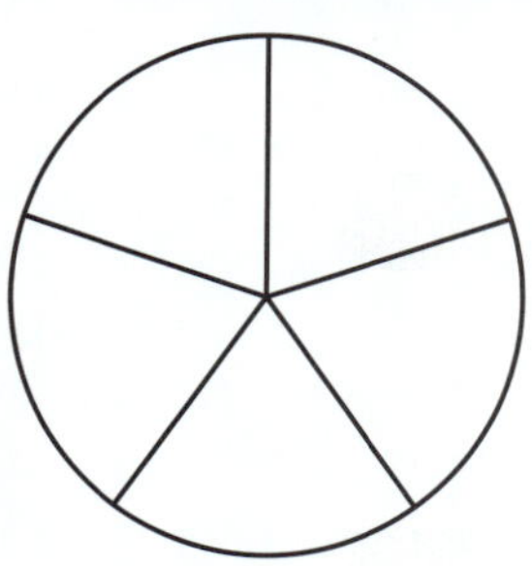

Continued

Count the number of parts in the circle. There are five equal parts. This is called the denominator and is the bottom number in the fraction.

Each part is one-fifth, $\frac{1}{5}$.

One-fifth of the circle is red, $\frac{1}{5}$

Two-fifths of the circle is blue, $\frac{2}{5}$

Two-fifths of the circle is green, $\frac{2}{5}$

The total number of parts coloured is five-fifths, $\frac{5}{5}$.

This is the same as one whole. The top number in a fraction is called the numerator. It tells you how many parts you have.

Exercise 7.1

1 Colour three parts green. Colour five parts yellow.

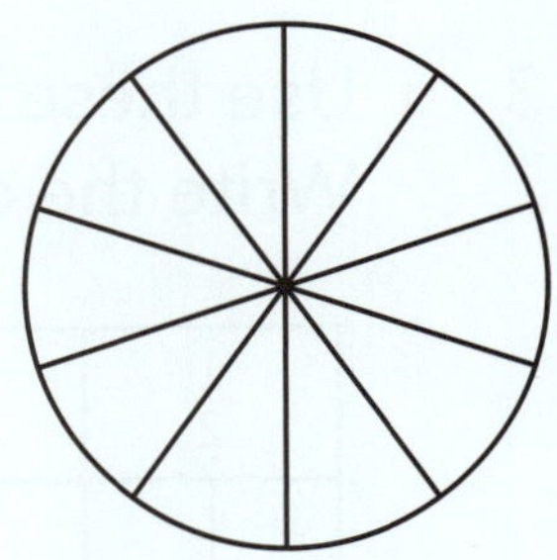

a What fraction of the circle is green?

____

b What fraction of the circle is yellow?

____

c What fraction of the circle is not coloured?

____

2 a If you and nine friends share the pizza, how many slices would you each get?

We would each get ______ slice(s).

b If you and four friends share the pizza, how many slices would you each get?

We would each get ______ slices.

c What is the fraction of the whole pizza that you would each get if:

- you and nine friends are sharing

  ______

- you and four friends are sharing?

  ______

3 a Use these fraction strips to find equivalent fractions. Write the correct fraction in the boxes.

$\frac{1}{2}$		$\frac{1}{2}$	

$\frac{1}{2} = \frac{\square}{4}$

$\frac{1}{5}$		$\frac{1}{5}$		$\frac{1}{5}$		$\frac{1}{5}$		$\frac{1}{5}$	

$\frac{1}{5} = \frac{\square}{10}$

b Draw your own fraction strips for quarters and halves and use them to find an equivalent fraction.

4 Some children make a poster about the fraction one-third.

Ask your teacher for a large piece of paper.

Choose a fraction and make your own fraction poster.

Show your fraction in as many different ways as you can.

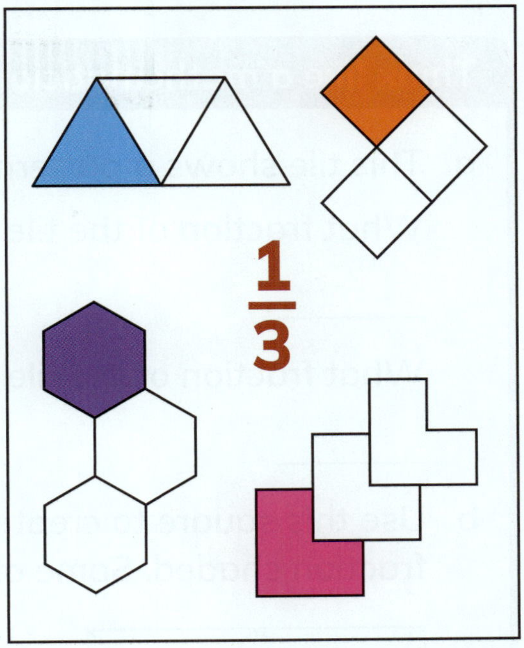

5 If this is $\frac{2}{4}$ of a shape, draw what the whole shape could look like.

Remember that your triangles must be the same size as these.

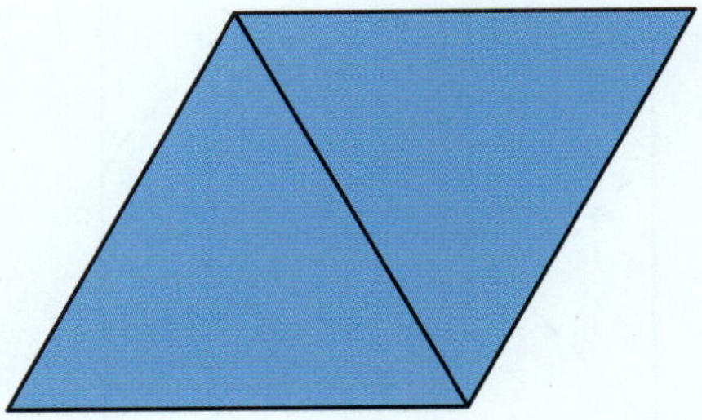

Think like a mathematician: Designing tiles

a This tile shows a pattern made with fractions.

What fraction of the tile is shaded?

____

What fraction of the tile is not shaded?

____

b Use this square to create a design with a different fraction shaded. Some of the dotted lines may help.

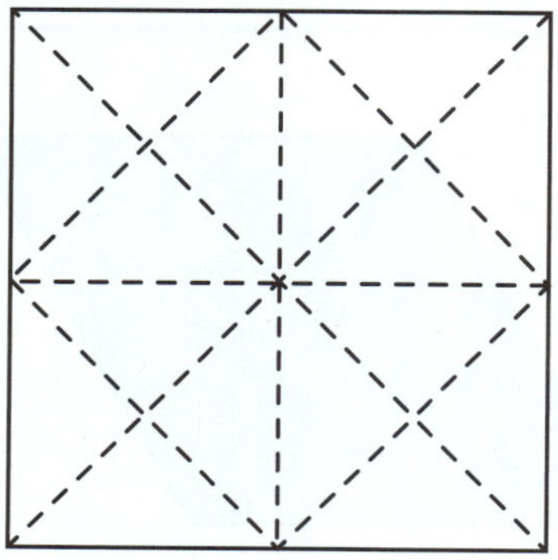

Design your own tile to show thirds or tenths.

Share your design with a partner. Ask them to find the fraction that is shaded and the fraction that has not been shaded.

What fraction did your partner use in their design? Explain how you know.

How can you check that your partner has shown their fraction correctly?

How many different designs could you make using the same fraction?

Look what I can do!

- ☐ I can explore fifths, thirds and tenths.
- ☐ I can show that two fractions can have equivalent values.
- ☐ I can explore the links between the whole and the parts.

Check your progress

1 a What fraction of the whole strip is shaded?
Draw a ring around your answer.

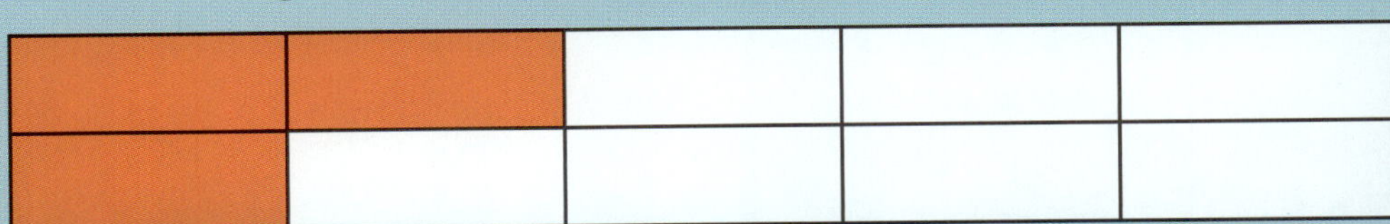

$\frac{3}{10}$ $\frac{7}{10}$ $\frac{3}{3}$ $\frac{1}{3}$

b If I shade two more boxes, how much is shaded now?
Draw a ring around your answer.

$\frac{2}{3}$ $\frac{2}{10}$ $\frac{1}{2}$ $\frac{1}{4}$

Continued

2 Count the number of sides in each shape.
For each shape, divide it into the same number of equal parts as the number of sides.
Colour two parts in each shape. What fractions are coloured?

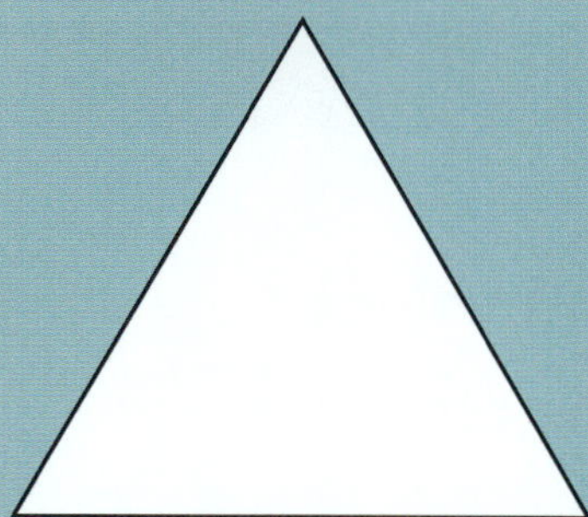

Number of sides: ______

Fraction that is coloured: ______

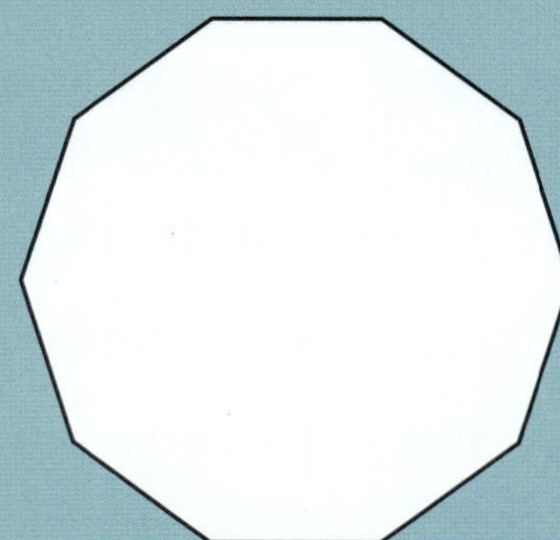

Number of sides: ______

Fraction that is coloured: ______

8 Time

Getting started

1 Write the correct times for each clock.

a 

____

b 

____

c 

____

d 

____

e 

____

In this unit, you will find out how analogue and digital clocks show the same time in different ways. You will work with the displays on both types of clocks. You will learn to tell the time to the minute.

8.1 Time

We are going to ...

- read and record time using analogue clocks
- read and record time using digital clocks
- link analogue and digital times.

Measuring time is part of everyone's life. Knowing the time can be useful when we need to catch a bus or a train. It will help us to get to school on time and to know when to leave school!

analogue clock
digital clock
minute

Worked example 1

On each of these clocks the minute hand is missing.

a 

b 

c 

Where should the minute hand be?

a 4 o'clock

If the hour hand is pointing exactly to a number, then it is an o'clock time and the minute hand points to 12.

b 28, 29, 30, 31 or 32 minutes past 8

If the hour hand is pointing about halfway between two numbers, then it is close to half past but may be one or two minutes to or from half past.

c 13, 14, 15, 16 or 17 minutes to 1

If the hour hand is pointing about three-quarters between two numbers, then it is close to 15 minutes to the next hour.

Exercise 8.1

1 On each of these clocks the minute hand is missing.

Working with a partner, estimate the time by finding where the minute hand should be.

a 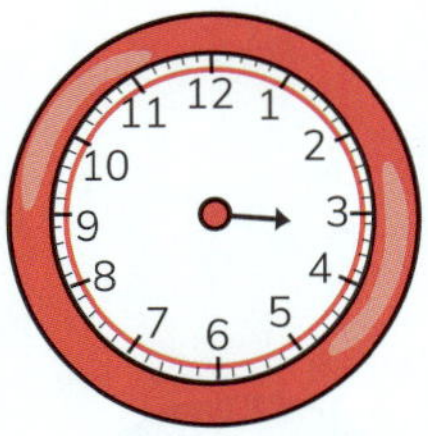

b 

c 

Estimate: ________ Estimate: ________ Estimate: ________

2 Write the time shown on these clocks.
The first one is done for you.

a 

quarter past 3 ____________

b 

____

c 

____

d 

____

e 

____

f 

____

3 Match the digital time to the analogue time that is shown on the clock.

a

b

c
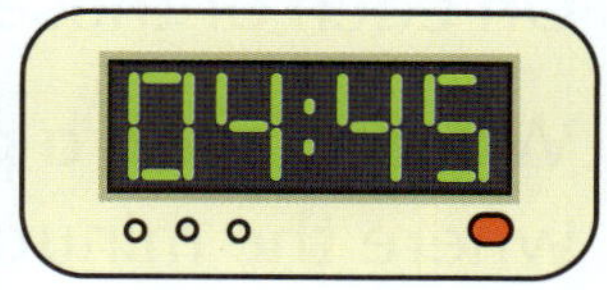

d

e

f

4 Choose three of your favourite times of day.
Show each time on an analogue clock and on a digital clock.

For each time, write what activity you are doing.

a
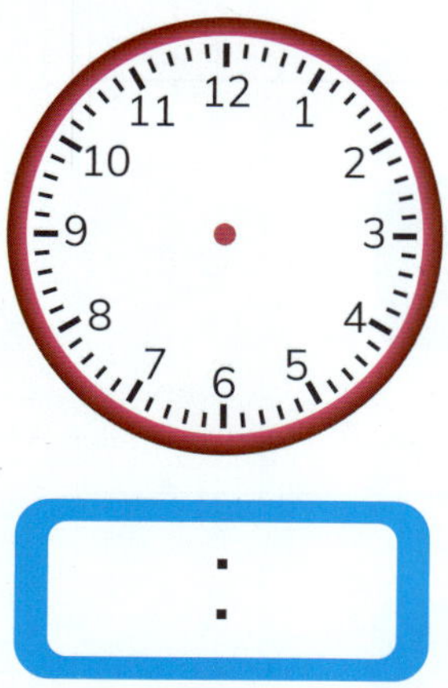

I am ____________

b
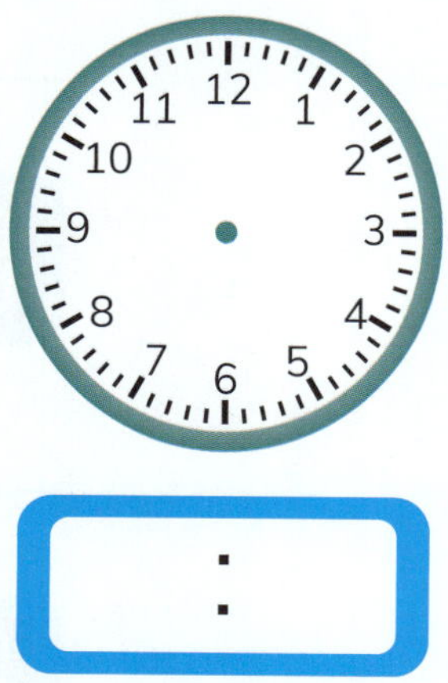

I am ____________

c
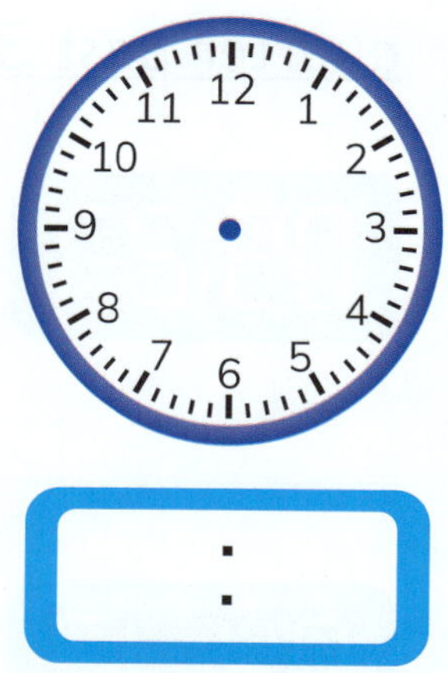

I am ____________

What time will it be 1 hour after each of your times? ____________

5 Write the times shown on these clocks.

a

____

b

____

c

____

d

____

Think like a mathematician

Work with a partner.

This digital stopwatch is broken.

a Every time it is switched on only five light bars work. What different numbers could it show?

____

b Investigate for other numbers of light bars. Is there a number of light bars that matches the number shown on the display? How many different numbers can you find that do that?

____

Can you explain to a partner how to write digital numbers?

Which type of clock do you like using the most? Why?

Look what I can do!

- ☐ I can read and record time using analogue clocks.
- ☐ I can read and record time using digital clocks.
- ☐ I can link analogue and digital times.

Check your progress

1 Write the time that is shown on each clock.

a

______

b

______

c

______

d

______

Continued

2 Write the time that is shown on each digital clock.

a 02:38 ______

b 05:09 ______

c 07:37 ______

d 06:15 ______

3 Change these written times to digital times.

a seven minutes past five

______

b twenty-four minutes to three

______

c twelve minutes to eleven

______

Continued

4 Which of these clocks shows a time that is between 8 o'clock and 10 o'clock? Place a circle around it.

a

b

c

d

Draw the hands of a clock to show two more times that are between 8 o'clock and 10 o'clock.

Write the times that you have made.

9 More addition and subtraction

Getting started

1 A library has 519 fiction and 348 non-fiction books. How many books are in the library all together? Estimate then calculate. Show your method.

2 A factory makes 375 T-shirts. A van collects 168 T-shirts at 3 o'clock. How many T-shirts are left in the factory? Estimate then calculate. Show your method.

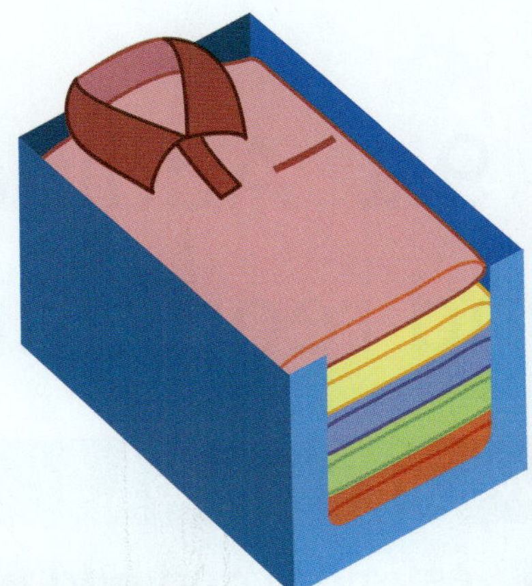

3 Xiang does the same subtraction in two different ways. His answers are different. Help Xiang to correct his mistakes.

estimate: 470 – 250 = 220

$$\begin{array}{rl} & 473 = 400 + 60 + 13 \\ - & 245 = \underline{200 + 40 + \;\;5} \\ & 200 + 20 + \;\;8 = 228 \end{array}$$

473 – 245
= 400 + 70 + 3 – 200 – 40 – 5
= 400 – 200 + 70 – 40 + 3 – 5
= 200 + 30 + 2 = 232

We all add and subtract every day, often without thinking about it. The way you add or subtract often depends on the numbers involved. This unit will continue to develop the methods that you use and help you to work mentally.

9.1 Addition: regrouping tens and reordering

We are going to ...

- estimate and add two 2-digit numbers, regrouping the tens or the ones
- estimate and add up to two 3-digit numbers, regrouping the tens or the ones
- reorder the numbers when adding, to support calculating.

You can already add some 3-digit numbers, regrouping the ones when you have too many for the ones place. In this unit you will find out how to add numbers with up to three digits, regrouping the tens when you have too many tens for the tens place.

associative
column addition
commutative

Exercise 9.1

1 Complete these 2-digit additions. Show your method.

a estimate:

43 + 56

=

b estimate:

67 + 29

=

2 Add together the two numbers represented below. Estimate the total. Complete the number sentence and represent the total in the place value grid.

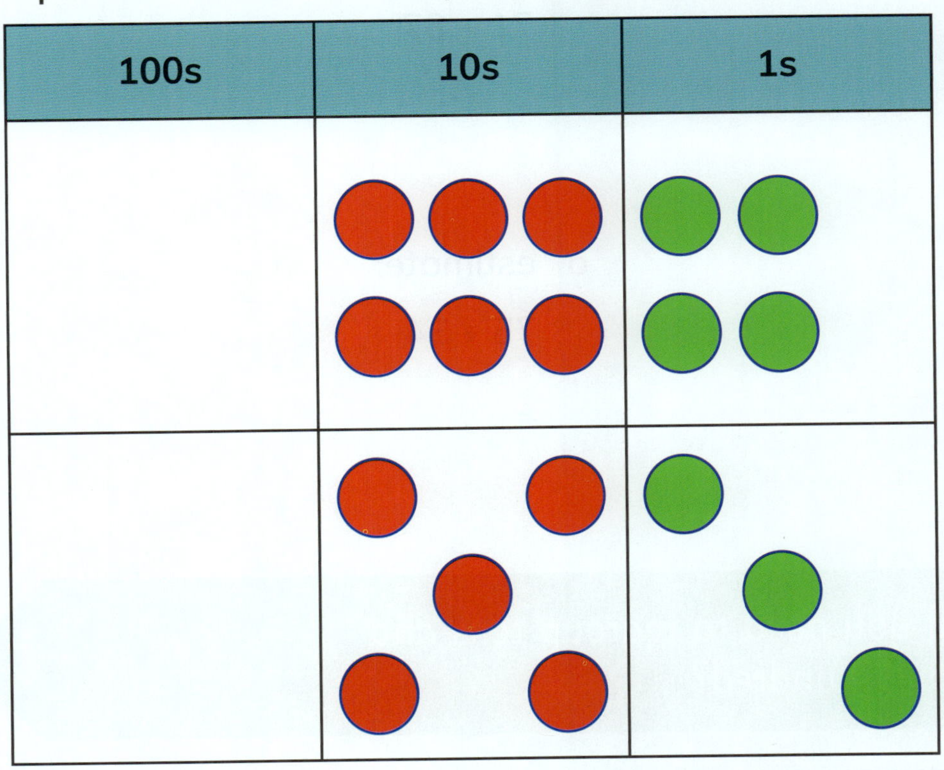

estimate: ____________

100s	10s	1s

☐ + ☐ = ☐

3 Estimate and then solve these 2-digit additions.
Show your method.

a estimate:

84 + 62

=

b estimate:

71 + 87

=

c estimate:

64 + 72

=

d estimate:

75 + 34

=

How do you know if you need to regroup tens and exchange 10 tens for 1 hundred?

Think like a mathematician

Marcus adds two 2-digit numbers. Their total is one hundred and thirty-seven. The ones digits were 6 and 1.
What could his numbers be?

Worked example 1

Estimate and then solve this addition. Show your method.

645 + 272

estimate: 650 + 270 650 + 270 = 920	Rounding to the nearest 10, 645 rounds to 650 and 272 rounds 270. I can count on in hundreds and tens from 650 to find the total estimate: 650, 750, 850, 860, 870, 880, 890, 900, 910, 920.
645 = 600 + 40 + 5 +272 = 200 + 70 + 2 800 + 110 + 7 = 917	I am going to decompose the numbers. Now I can add the hundreds, tens and ones together and compose the total.

4 Estimate and then solve these additions. Show your method.

a estimate:

233 + 50

=

b estimate:

178 + 60

=

c estimate:

154 + 65

=

d estimate:

191 + 56

=

e estimate:

286 + 352

=

f estimate:

473 + 166

=

Share and discuss your methods with your partner.

5

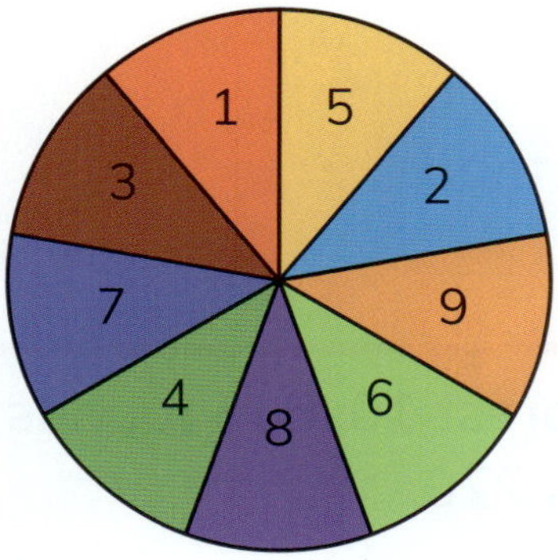

You will need a paper clip and a pencil to use the spinner.

Spin the spinner three times to find three single-digit numbers. Add them. Show your method.

Now spin the spinner four times to find four single-digit numbers to add. Show your method.

Why did you add your numbers in the way that you did? Share and discuss your reasons with your partner. Are some methods more efficient than others? What is the most efficient method? Explain why.

6 Choose three different 3-digit numbers to add by reading across or reading down the grid. Estimate and then solve your addition. Show your method.

1	3	2
2	5	3
3	4	1

Explain to your partner why you chose to add your numbers in the way that you did.

7 Record in words any two numbers from question 6. How is the place value of a number shown in words and in numbers?

Look what I can do!

- [ ] I can estimate and add two 2-digit numbers, regrouping the tens or the ones.
- [ ] I can estimate and add up to two 3-digit numbers, regrouping the tens or the ones.
- [ ] I can reorder the numbers when I am adding, to support calculating.

9.2 Subtraction: regrouping tens

We are going to ...

- estimate and subtract a 2-digit number from a 3-digit number, regrouping the tens or the ones
- estimate and subtract a 3-digit number from a 3-digit number, regrouping the tens or the ones
- use trial and improvement to find an unknown number.

You can already subtract ones from a 3-digit number, regrouping a ten as 10 ones when you don't have enough ones in the ones place to subtract from. In this unit you will find out how to subtract numbers with up to three digits when you don't have enough tens in the tens place to subtract from.

exchange regroup
trial and improvement
unknown

Exercise 9.2

1 Regroup each number by exchanging 1 hundred for 10 tens.
The first one is done for you.

a 235 = 100 + 130 + 5

b 452 =

c 763 =

d 309 =

2 Estimate the answer.
Solve and represent your answer in the place value grid.

estimate:

246 – 84 =

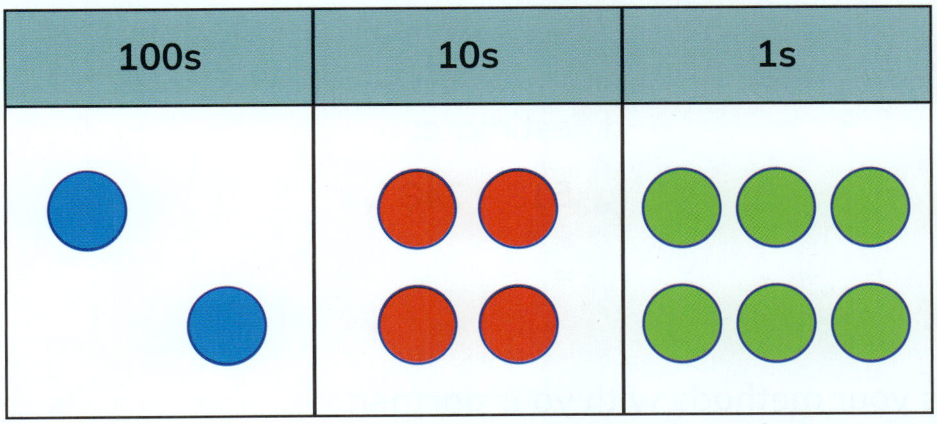

↓

100s	10s	1s

3 Estimate and then solve these subtractions. Show your method.

a estimate:

148 – 60

=

b estimate:

245 – 82

=

c estimate:

326 – 71

=

d estimate:

534 – 93

=

Share and discuss your methods with your partner.

4 Estimate and then solve these subtractions. Show your method.

a estimate:

339 – 163

=

b estimate:

355 – 172

=

c estimate:

647 – 386

=

d estimate:

518 – 248

=

Share and discuss your methods with your partner.
Did you use different methods in questions 3 and 4?

Check two of your subtractions in question 4 using a different calculation.

Worked example 2

Find the unknown value, using trial and improvement.
The unknown value is represented by a smiley face.

There are 147 adults and children at the museum.
If 63 of them are adults, how many children are at the museum?

147 –  = 63

There must be fewer than 100 children.

Find a starting point that gives you an idea of the sort of number you are looking for.

147 – 47 is 100 and I need to subtract a bit more.

63 – 47 is 16, so I need to subtract another 16.

Improve your calculation by making a small change.

100 – 16 = 84

 = 84, so there are 84 children at the museum.

Find the solution to the problem.

5 Find the unknown value, using trial and improvement.

a There are 243 adults and children in the park.
If 151 of them are children, how many adults are there?

243 –  = 151

So  =

b Sofia and Zara have 34 marbles all together.
They both have the same number of marbles.
How many marbles do they have each?
Each bag of marbles represents the unknown value.

 +  = 34

So  = □

Think like a mathematician

△ and □ represent unknown digits.

3△7 – 1□7 = 160

What could the values of △ and □ be?

Are △ and □ both odd, both even, or is one odd and one even? Why?

Talk with your partner about how you carried out your investigation. Compare your methods and results.

Would you use the same methods if you did another similar investigation?

Look what I can do!

- ☐ I can estimate and subtract a 2-digit number from a 3-digit number, regrouping the tens or the ones.
- ☐ I can estimate and subtract a 3-digit number from a 3-digit number, regrouping the tens or the ones.
- ☐ I can use trial and improvement to find an unknown number.

9.3 Complements

We are going to ...

- find complements of 100 and 1000 (using multiples of 10)
- find complements of multiples of 10 or 100 up to 1000
- calculate estimates mentally.

As numbers get larger, counting on or counting back is not efficient. For numbers that are multiples of 10, it is better to calculate mentally using known number bonds.

blank
complement
mentally

Exercise 9.3

1 Find the complements of 100. Use the blank 100 square and what you know about number facts for 10 to help you.

a 35 + ☐ = 100

b 53 + ☐ = 100

c 77 + ☐ = 100

d 81 + ☐ = 100

e 8 + ☐ = 100

How does the blank 100 square help you find complements of 100?

2 Continue the pattern of complements of 1000.

500 + 500
510 + 490

Check your pattern of complements with your partner. Discuss the methods that you used. Did you use the same or different methods?

3 Make each addition fact in question 1 ten times larger to make complements of 1000 that are multiples of 10.

a 35 + ☐ = 100 → 350 + ☐ = 1000

b 53 + ☐ = 100 →

c 77 + ☐ = 100 →

d 81 + ☐ = 100 →

e 8 + ☐ = 100 →

4 Find the missing complements. Remember to calculate mentally.

a 880 + ☐ = 1000

b 470 + ☐ = 1000

c 240 + ☐ = 1000

d 510 + ☐ = 1000

e 340 + ☐ = 570

f 750 + ☐ = 900

g 560 + ☐ = 850

h 370 + ☐ = 720

i 670 + ☐ = 810

j 390 + ☐ = 570

Marcus says that calculating is much easier and quicker than counting on or counting back. Do you agree? Explain why.

5 Here are Rojeeta's estimate calculations. Complete the calculations for her. Remember to calculate mentally to find the answers.

a $980 - 260 = \square$

b $740 - 340 = \square$

c $670 - 380 = \square$

e $810 - 520 = \square$

f $760 - 490 = \square$

g $520 - 370 = \square$

h $850 - 480 = \square$

i $630 - 470 = \square$

Discuss with your partner how you calculated the estimates in question 5. Did you use the same or different methods? Would you use the same methods if you did another similar investigation?

Think like a mathematician

Arun adds two 3-digit multiples of ten. His total is 540. Sofia says that there are 35 possible pairs of numbers that Arun could have added. Do you agree? Why?

Look what I can do!

- ☐ I can find complements of 100 and 1000 (using multiples of 10).
- ☐ I can find complements of multiples of 10 or 100 up to 1000.
- ☐ I can calculate estimates mentally.

Check your progress

1 Calculate your estimate then solve these calculations.
Show your method.

a estimate:

263 + 174

=

b estimate:

475 + 353

=

c estimate:

358 – 187

=

d estimate:

736 – 472

=

2 Ebele finds some complements of 100 and 1000.
Check Ebele's work and correct any mistakes.

Number	Complement of 100
54	46
19	91
77	33

Number	Complement of 1000
440	660
753	247
288	722

3 Complete Omar's estimate calculations. Remember to calculate mentally to find the answers.

a 370 + 290 = ☐

b 550 + 180 = ☐

c 670 – 290 = ☐

d 740 – 460 = ☐

e 370 + ☐ = 730

f 820 – ☐ = 470

10 Graphs

Getting started

1 Use the data on the pictogram to help you answer the questions.

Animals in the zoo

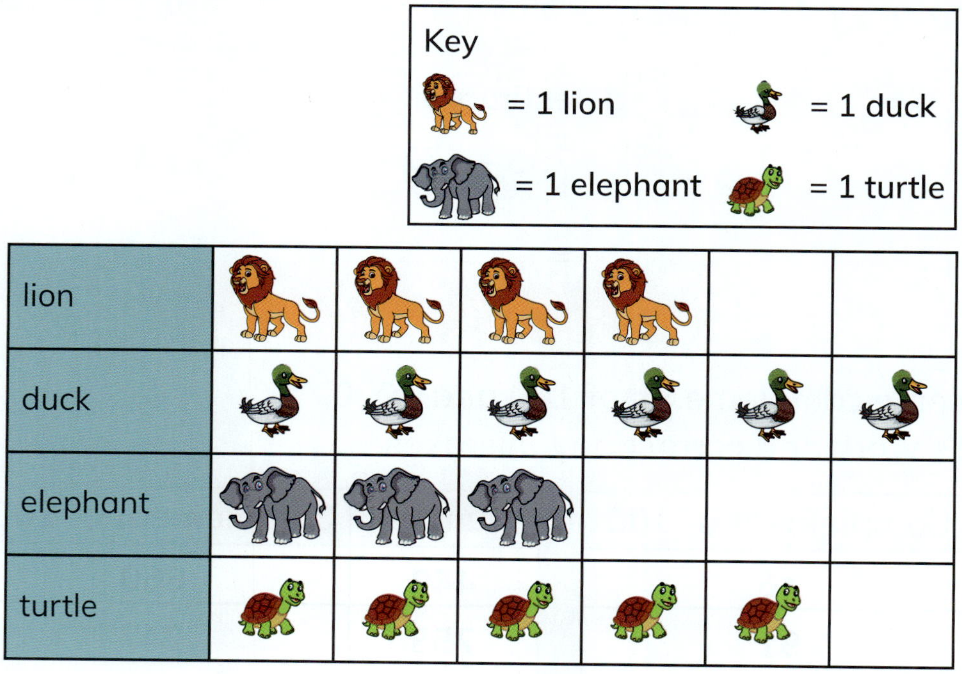

a How many ducks are there? ☐

b How many elephants are there? ☐

c How many more turtles than elephants are there? ☐

d How many animals are there all together? ☐

e How many fewer lions than ducks are there? ☐

There are four main steps in an investigation:

1 Decide what question you want to answer and plan how will find the answer.

2 Collect your data and record it.

3 Look at the data and work out what it shows.

4 Look back at your question. Does the data answer it?

This is the process that all statisticians follow.

In this unit, we are going to look at more ways to record data. We are also going to practise looking at data and working out what it shows.

10.1 Pictograms and bar charts

We are going to ...

- record, organise and represent data using pictograms and bar charts
- interpret data, finding things that are the same and things that are different, asking and answering questions.

axes axis
discrete data
represent

You can use a pictogram as a visual tally, using pictures instead of bars to compare data. Pictograms work best when pictures are simple enough to understand.

Food I like

Bar charts use bars to compare data. They use two axes: one is vertical and one is horizontal.

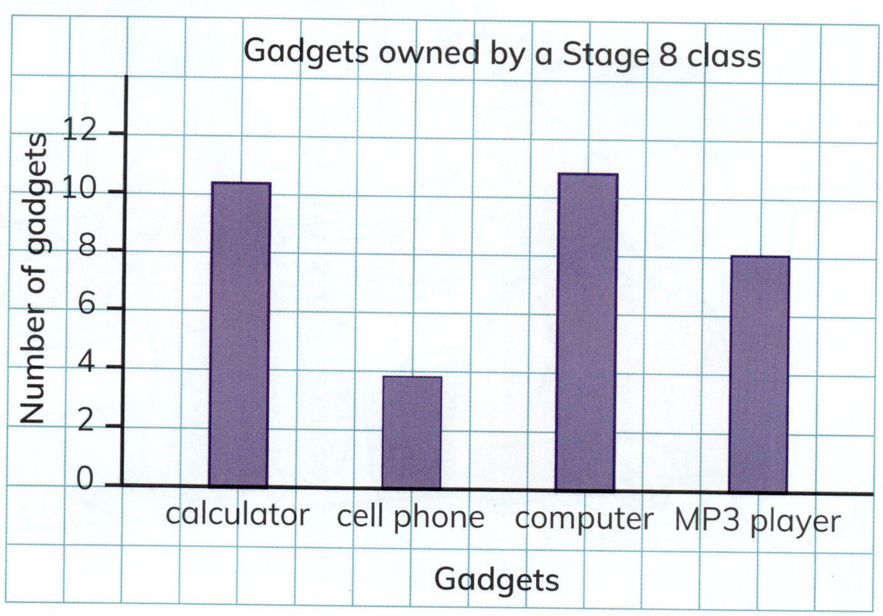

Worked example 1

On which day did it rain the most?

Rainy days

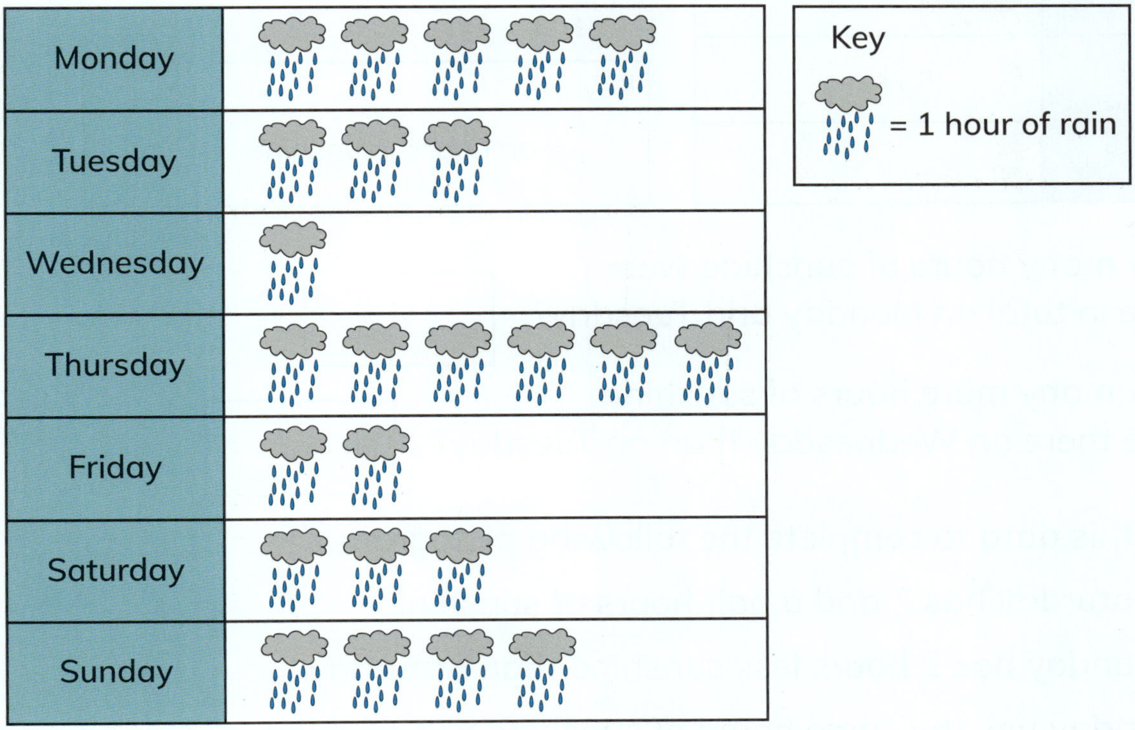

It rained the most on Thursday because the data shows more rain clouds.

It rained for 6 hours because the key tells us that  = 1 hour of rain.

Exercise 10.1

1 **Hours of sunshine**

Key

 = an hour of sunshine

a How many hours of sunshine were there in total on Monday and Tuesday?

b How many more hours of sunshine were there on Wednesday than on Tuesday?

c Use this data to complete the following pictogram.

- Saturday has 7 and a half hours of sunshine.
- Sunday has 2 hours less sunshine than Saturday.
- Friday has the same hours of sunshine as Saturday and Sunday added together.

Title:

Friday	
Saturday	
Sunday	

Key

2 a Use this data to complete the bar chart.
Give the bar chart a title and labels.

The pet shop has one turtle, three rabbits, six fish, eight cats and nine guinea pigs.

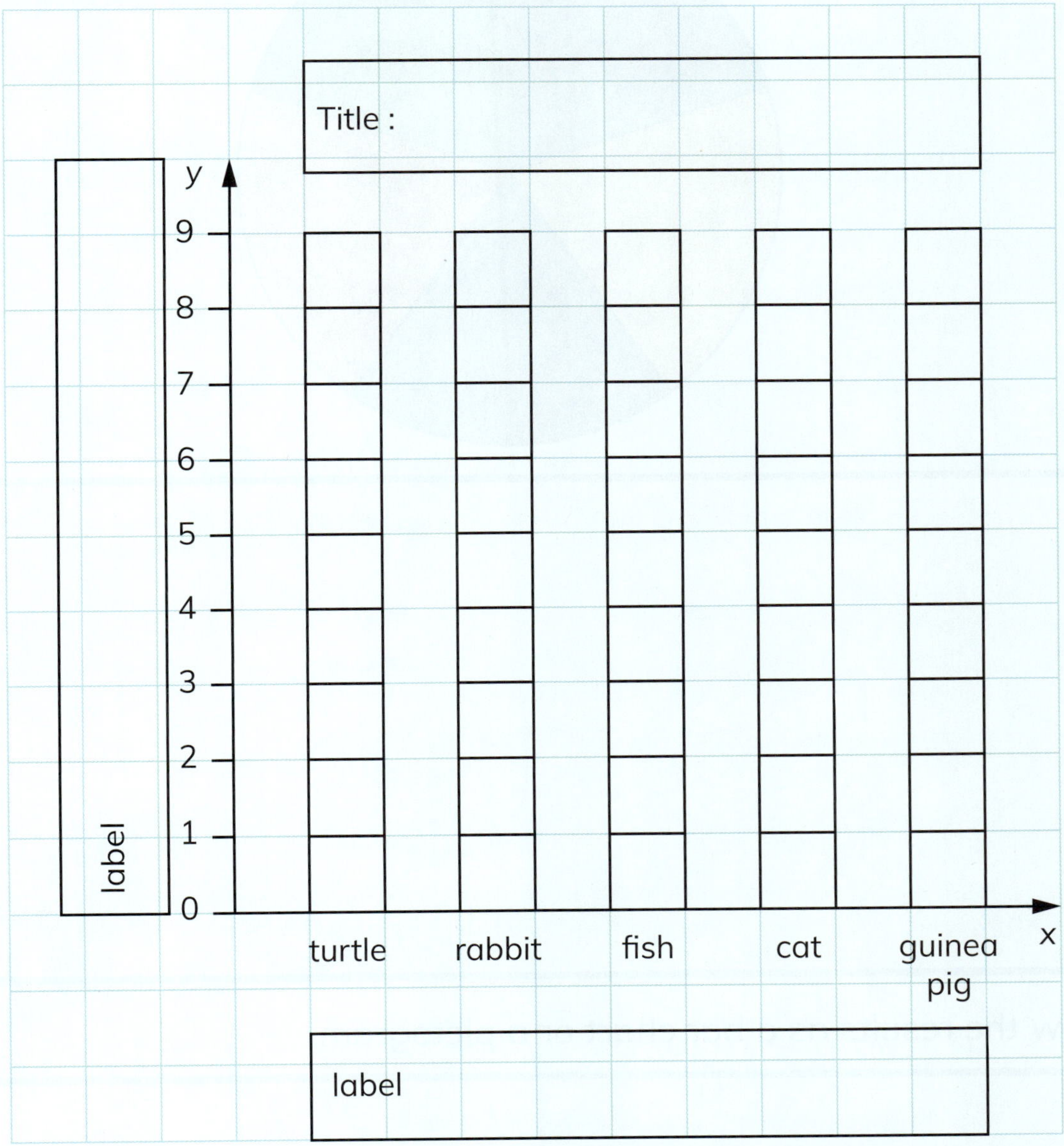

b Use the data on your bar chart to write two questions for your partner to answer.

1 ____________________

2 ____________________

3 a Use a paperclip with the spinner. Spin it 20 times.
Record the results.

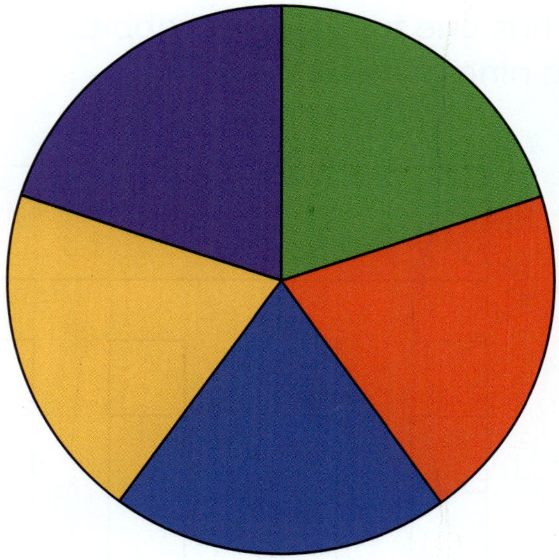

b Show the results as a bar chart or a pictogram.

c Compare your results with a partner's results.
What is the same? What is different?

____

____

d Why did you choose that way of representing the data?

____

____

e Use the data on your graph to write two questions for your partner to answer.

1 ____

2 ____

4 a Ask five friends, and yourself, for the number of letters in their first name.

b Decide which method of recording your data will be best, then record it here.

c What did you find out?

d Write three sentences about your data.

1 ____

2 ____

3 ____

5 Work within a group.

Choose one of these questions to investigate:

1 Where would you like to visit?

2 Where would you go for a day with your best friend?

3 What would you do if school was closed?

4 What would you take on a picnic?

My group chose this question: ______________________________

Now think of four possible options in response to the question. Write them in the first column of the table.

Which answers do you think will be the most popular?

____

Do a class survey and collect the results in a tally chart.

Options	Tally	Frequency

How else can you show the information?

____

____

Explain your choice.

____

____

Think like a mathematician

You will need two six-sided dice and a partner.

If you throw the two dice together 20 times, how many times do you think you will throw a total of 7? Discuss with your partner.

You are now going to test your idea. Decide how you will record your results.

Throw the dice together 20 times and record the totals.

Look at your data. Does it match what you thought would happen? Discuss with your partner.

What do you think will happen if you carry out the investigation again?

Did you ask questions if you needed help during your investigation? Did you check your work for mistakes?

Look what I can do!

- ☐ I can record, organise and represent data using pictograms and bar charts.
- ☐ I can interpret data, finding things that are the same and things that are different, asking and answering questions.

10.2 Venn and Carroll diagrams

We are going to ...

- record, organise and show data using Venn and Carroll diagrams
- interpret data, finding things that are the same and things that are different, asking and answering questions.

A Venn diagram shows lots of information. Making a Venn diagram is simple. You just need circles, data and a box to put them in.

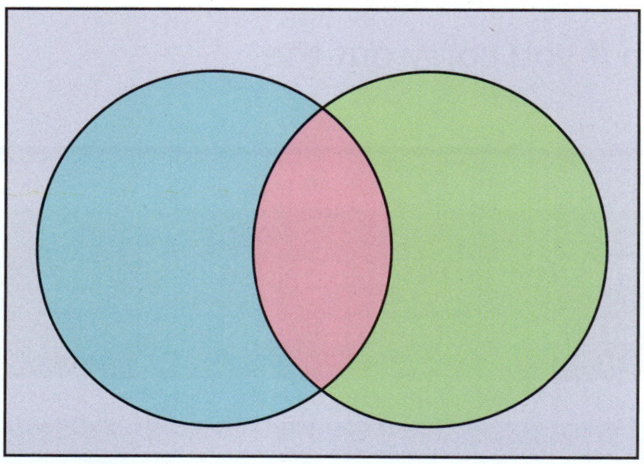

Carroll diagram
Venn diagram

A Venn diagram shows the relationship between a group of different things (a set) in a visual way.

A Carroll diagram is another visual way to organise and group data using rules.

	Curves	Not curves
Blue		
Not blue		

Worked example 2

Write these ten numbers in the correct place in the Venn diagram.

68 79 56 53 121 24 96 59 76

Use the overlap to show numbers that have both characteristics.
Use the circles to show what is different.

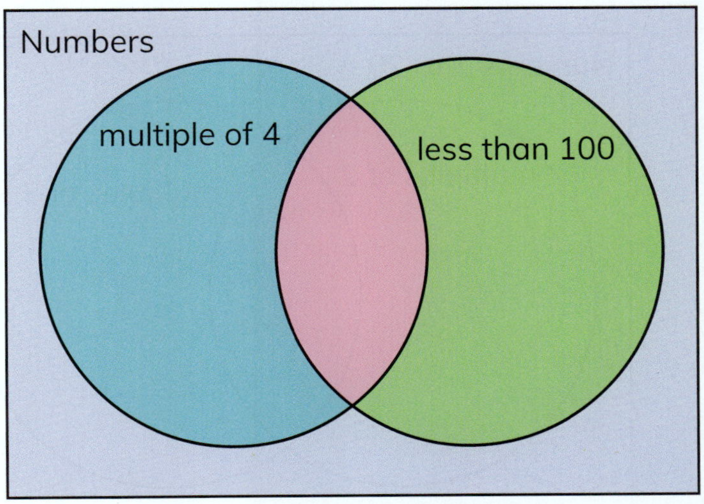

First, sort the numbers that are multiples of 4.

What is left is not a multiple of 4. If any of these are more than 100, they are written in the box. If they are less than 100, they are written in the right circle.

Multiples of 4 that are also less than 100 are written in the overlap.

The remaining numbers go into the left circle.

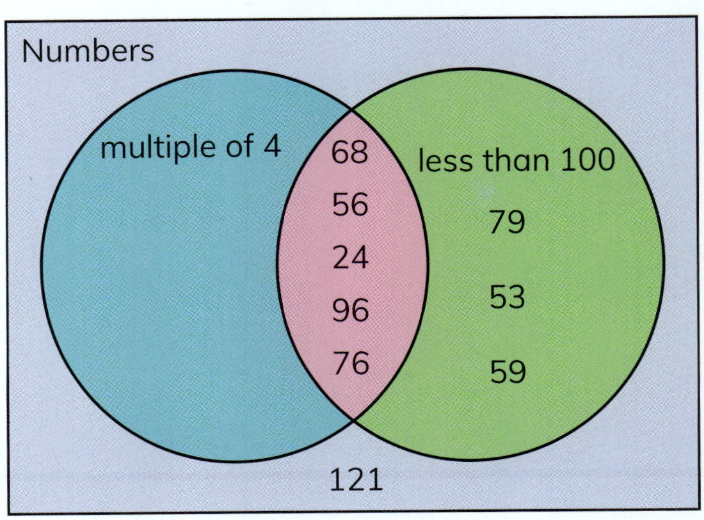

Exercise 10.2

1 a Complete this Venn diagram for the numbers 1 to 20.

Cross out the numbers to make sure that you have used them all.

1 2 3 4 5 6 7 8 9 10 11 12 13 14 15 16 17 18 19 20

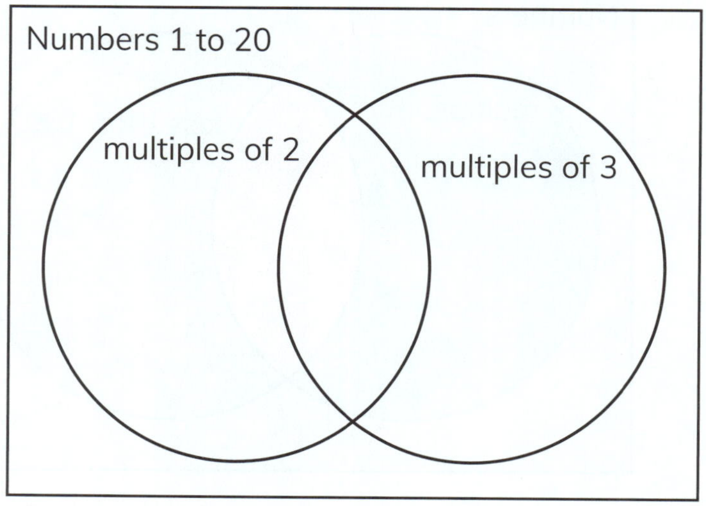

b Choose a set of 12 numbers. Draw a Venn diagram. Label it and sort your numbers.

2 a Use the numbers in the list and fill the Carroll diagram.

15 11 10 16 18 21 20 22 12 24 17 23

	Even	Not even
Multiple of 3		
Not a multiple of 3		

b Choose a set of 12 numbers.
Draw a Carroll diagram.
Label it and sort your numbers.

3 Work as a group of four to make a Venn diagram.

a Decide on a question to ask each other.

b Join with another group of four. Ask everyone the same question.

c Collect the data that you need from both groups.

d Show the data in a Venn diagram.

e Write three things that you can find out from the diagram.

1 ____________________

2 ____________________

3 ____________________

4 The monsters have arrived. They are your data.

With a partner, organise and group the monsters into the Carroll diagram.

Write the labels.

Swap your diagram with another pair of learners.
Did they choose the same rules as you? Is their diagram correct?

Think like a mathematician

Make a poster to show all the ways of recording data that you know. Explain when you would use each method.

Did you use all the correct words?
Would the monsters understand the poster?

Look what I can do!

- ☐ I can record, organise and show data using Venn and Carroll diagrams.
- ☐ I can interpret data, finding things that are the same and things that are different, asking and answering questions.

Check your progress

1 Sort the monsters into groups by counting their legs.

a Complete the pictogram.

Two legs				
Three legs				
Four legs				

b Look at the pictogram and write two things that you see.

1 ____________________

2 ____________________

c How else could you sort the monsters?

____

2 Sort these shapes into the Carroll diagram.
(Draw the shapes or write the names.)

	Has vertices	**Does not have vertices**
2D		
Not 2D		

Continued

3 Sort these numbers into the Venn diagram.
10 25 8 5 31 17 35 16 40 19 29

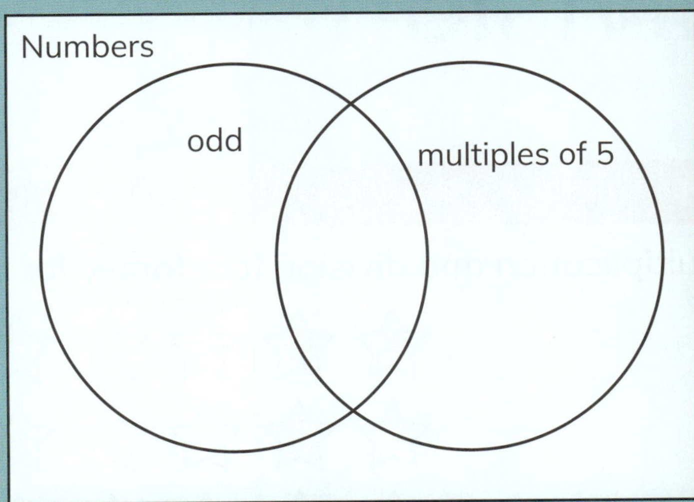

4 This bar chart shows the result when a six-sided dice is rolled 20 times.

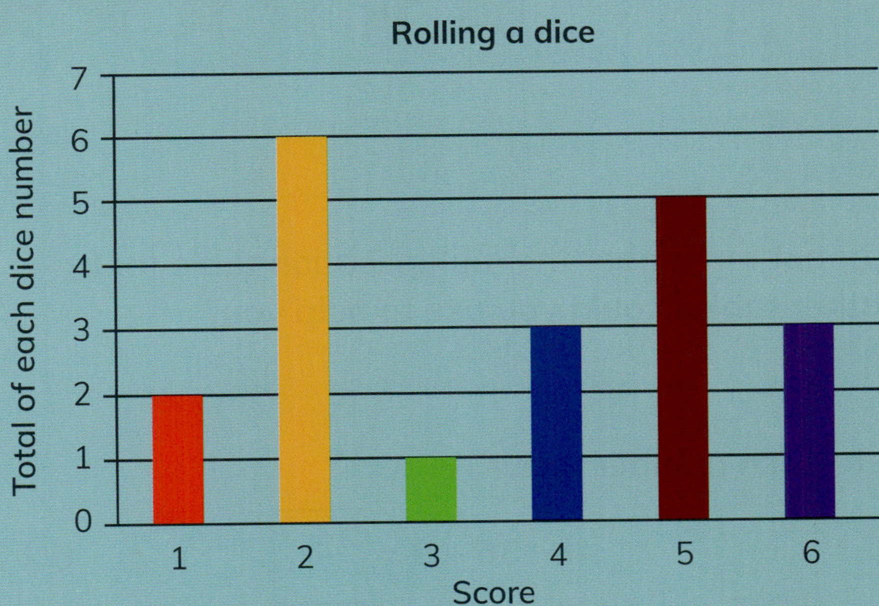

a How many times is 4 rolled? ☐

b Write two more things that you know by looking at the bar chart.

1 ____________________

2 ____________________

11 More multiplication and division

Getting started

1 Write the multiplication and division fact family for this array.

2 If you cannot remember the multiplication table for 8, which other tables could you use to help you?

3 Complete each number fact.

a $8 \times 3 = \square$

b $36 \div 9 = \square$

c $6 \times 7 = \square$

d $5 \times 10 = \square$

e $60 \div 6 = \square$

f $13 \times 10 = \square$

g $9 \times 8 = \square$

h $8 \div 4 = \square$

i $0 \times 5 = \square$

You will often need to multiply or divide. There are a lot of multiplication facts to remember, but there are not as many as you think.

This unit will introduce you to the multiplication square and all its patterns. You will also find out how to reorder multiplications to make the calculations easier, as well as how to multiply and divide with larger numbers.

11.1 Revisiting multiplication and division

We are going to ...

- make a multiplication square
- find out how to read the multiplication and division facts in a multiplication square
- use a multiplication square to make sequences of numbers.

A multiplication square helps you to see all of the products in one place. You will use a multiplication square to help you find multiplication and division facts, fact families and sequences. There are many patterns in the multiplication tables.

commutative
diagonal line
extend product

Exercise 11.1

1 Write the missing products in the empty squares.

×	1	2	3	4	5	6	7	8	9	10
1										
2										
3										
4										
5										
6										
7										
8										
9										
10										

2 When you draw a diagonal line on the multiplication square, from the multiplication symbol in the top left-hand corner to the bottom right-hand corner, what can you say about the products that the line passes through?

____

____

3 Read along the row and column from each product in question 1 to find the group size and quotient for a division calculation.

Write the division calculations that you find.

Think like a mathematician

Which numbers are shown on the multiplication square only once? Explain why.

How did you carry out your investigation? Explain to a partner what you did and listen to your partner's explanation of what they did. Would you use the same methods if you did another similar investigation?

4 Use a multiplication grid to help you find the numbers in the fact families for 28 and 72. Write each fact family.

Why is multiplication commutative but division is not commutative?

5 Extend each sequence.
What is the term-to-term rule for each sequence?

a 18, 27, 36, 45, ☐, ☐, ☐.

The term-to-term rule is ______________.

b 18, 23, 28, 33, ☐, ☐, ☐.

The term-to-term rule is ______________.

c 83, 91, 99, 107, ☐, ☐, ☐.

The term-to-term rule is ______________.

d 135, 126, 117, 108, ☐, ☐, ☐.

The term-to-term rule is ______________.

6 The term-to-term rule is subtract 8. Start at 108.
What are the next five numbers in the sequence?

108, ☐, ☐, ☐, ☐, ☐.

Look what I can do!

- ☐ I can make a multiplication square.
- ☐ I know how to read the multiplication and division facts in a multiplication square.
- ☐ I can use a multiplication square to make sequences of numbers.

11.2 Playing with multiplication and division

We are going to ...

- multiply numbers in any order
- multiply numbers up to 20 by 2, 3, 4 or 5
- find out how to record what is left over after division.

Multiplication is commutative, just like addition. You can multiply in any order, so you can reorder a calculation to simplify it. Division sometimes leaves part of the whole left over. You will find out how to show that in your calculation.

distributive property
quotient remainder
simplify

Exercise 11.2

1 Multiply each set of three numbers in any order to simplify the calculation and find the product.

a $5 \times 4 \times 3$

b $6 \times 5 \times 3$

c $6 \times 4 \times 2$

d $8 \times 3 \times 2$

Tip

Remember, multiplication is commutative, you can multiply numbers together in any order you choose.

2 Choose one of the sets of numbers from question 1. Simplify the calculation in a different way to check that the product is the same.

Sofia says that the fact that addition and multiplication are commutative is very useful. Do you agree? Why?

Worked example 1

Simplify this multiplication to help you find the product.

$16 \times 4 =$

Multiplication is distributive. Split the number you want to multiply into smaller pieces. Multiply each piece and add the products together to find the answer.

$$16 \times 4 = \begin{array}{r} 10 \times 4 = 40 \\ + \\ 6 \times 4 = \underline{24} \\ \underline{64} \end{array}$$

Marcus says, 'I split 16 into 10 and 6. I multiplied each number by 4, then added them together. 16 × 4 = 64.'

$$16 \times 4 = \begin{array}{r} 8 \times 4 = 32 \\ + \\ 8 \times 4 = \underline{32} \\ \underline{64} \end{array}$$

Arun says, 'I split 16 into 8 and 8. I needed to only multiply by 4 once because they are the same. I doubled 32. 16 × 6 = 64.'

Both methods work, well done!

3 Simplify each multiplication to help you find the product.

a 13 × 4 =

b 18 × 5 =

c 12 × 2 =

d 15 × 3 =

Marcus says that the fact that multiplication is distributive is fun because he can use the multiplication facts that he knows to help him find new facts in lots of different ways.

Do you agree with Marcus? Why?

4 Complete each division. Make sure that you include any remainders.

a $28 \div 4 =$ ☐ b $25 \div 2 =$ ☐ c $53 \div 5 =$ ☐

d $32 \div 4 =$ ☐ e $10 \div 4 =$ ☐ f $46 \div 3 =$ ☐

5 Four children share a bag of 30 sweets between them equally. How many sweets does each child get?

Write the division calculation that shows the result.

Think like a mathematician

Find a number between 10 and 20 that always leaves a remainder when you divide by 2, 3, 4 and 5.

Check with a friend. Did you find the same number?

How did you carry out your investigation?
Talk to a friend about what they did.
Would you use the same methods if you did another similar investigation?

Look what I can do!

- [ ] I can multiply numbers in any order.
- [ ] I can multiply numbers up to 20 by 2, 3, 4 or 5.
- [ ] I know how to record the remainder after division.

11.3 Extending multiplication and division

We are going to ...

- estimate and multiply numbers up to 100 by 2, 3, 4 and 5
- estimate and divide numbers up to 100 by 2, 3, 4 and 5
- find out what a remainder means in a problem.

In this section, you will extend the numbers that you work with when multiplying and dividing. You will also explore what the remainder after division represents. Sometimes you will need to round up the answer by 1, depending on the problem.

approach
interpret

Exercise 11.3

Worked example 2

Estimate the product of 27 × 4. Record the multiplication calculation in a grid and find the product.

estimate: 30 × 4 = 120

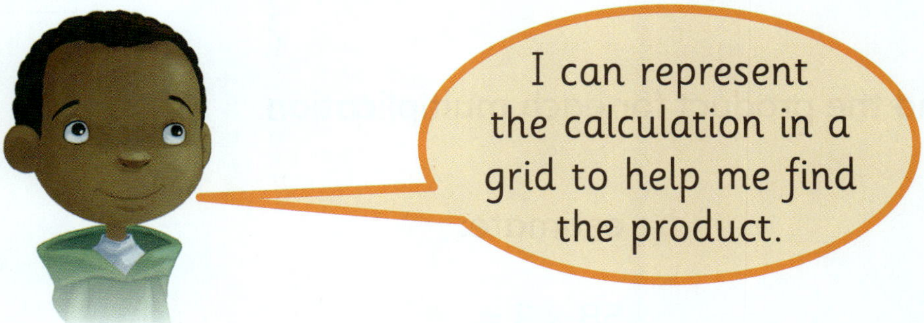

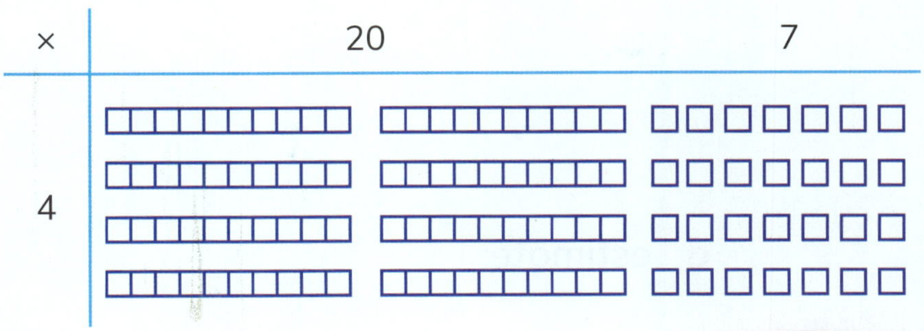

80 + 28 = 108

27 × 4 = 108

×	20	7
4	80	28

80 + 28 = 108

27 × 4 = 108

1 Estimate the product of 23 × 4. Record the multiplication calculation in the grid and find the product.

estimate:

×	

2 Estimate and then find the product for each multiplication. Use the grid method.

a estimate:

35 × 4 =

b estimate:

58 × 3 =

c estimate:

94 × 2 =

d estimate:

76 × 5 =

If you were not using the grid method in question 2, which method would you use for each calculation? Why?

3 Choose a number from the table.
Spin the spinner to find out whether to divide by 2, 3, 4 or 5.
Remember to estimate before you calculate. Do this twice.

87	43	29
49	59	73
61	38	65

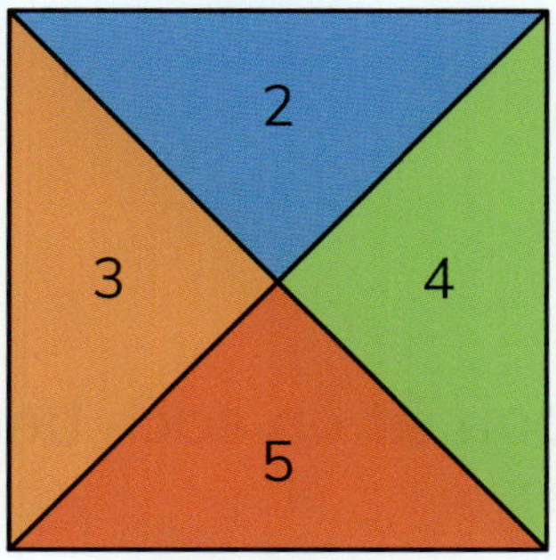

Arun says that estimating a division is harder than estimating a multiplication. What advice can you give to Arun to help him?

Think like a mathematician

Find a number that is less than 100 that can be divided by 2, 3, 4 and 5 with no remainder.

4 There are 46 tennis balls. Four tennis balls fit into each tube.
How many tubes are needed for 46 balls? Show your method.

5 There are 36 marbles in a set. Five children are playing. How many marbles do they get each? Show your method.

6 Ten children can sit on each bench.

How many benches are needed to seat 37 children? Show your method.

7 Make up a word problem for these divisions.

a $31 \div 4 = 7$ r3

b $77 \div 3 = 25$ r2

Look what I can do!

- ☐ I can estimate and multiply numbers up to 100 by 2, 3, 4 and 5.
- ☐ I can estimate and divide numbers up to 100 by 2, 3, 4 and 5.
- ☐ I understand what a remainder means in a problem.

Check your progress

1 Roll two 1 to 6 dice. Make a 2-digit number.
Multiply your number by three. Estimate before you calculate.

2 Roll two 1 to 6 dice. Make a 2-digit number.
Divide your number by five. Estimate before you calculate.
Remember to show any remainder.

3 Wenkai's calculation is $37 \div 3 = 12$ r1.
What word problem could he have been solving?
Is 13 the correct answer to the problem?

Continued

4 Which division will give the greater answer? How do you know?

$72 \div 4$ $72 \div 3$

12 More fractions

Getting started

1 What fraction of each shape is shaded?
Tick the correct fraction below each shape.

a

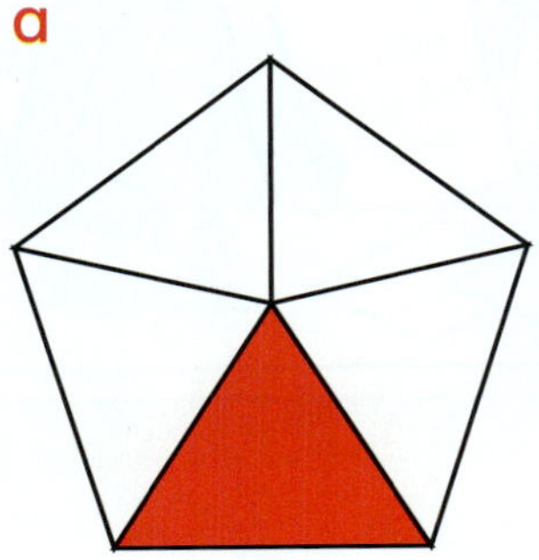

$\frac{1}{2}$ $\frac{1}{3}$ $\frac{1}{4}$ $\frac{1}{5}$ $\frac{1}{10}$

b

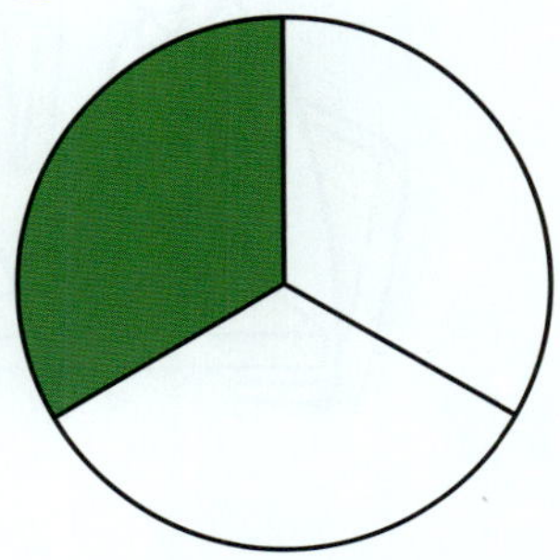

$\frac{1}{2}$ $\frac{1}{3}$ $\frac{1}{4}$ $\frac{1}{5}$ $\frac{1}{10}$

c

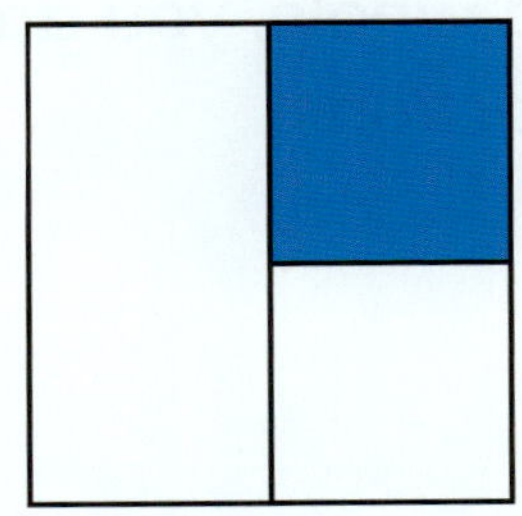

$\frac{1}{2}$ $\frac{1}{3}$ $\frac{1}{4}$ $\frac{1}{5}$ $\frac{1}{10}$

2 Kwame says that $\frac{1}{10}$ of a whole is greater than $\frac{1}{5}$ of the same whole because 10 is greater than 5.
Do you agree with Kwame?

3 A large pizza has ten equal slices.
Mum and Dad eat $\frac{2}{5}$ of the pizza each,
Hinata eats the rest.
How many slices does each person eat?

____

What fraction of the pizza does Hinata eat?

____

In this unit, you will link fractions and division to help you find fractions of numbers and some measures. You will also order and compare fractions, as well as add and subtract them. Whenever you find an equal part of a whole, you are using fractions!

12.1 Fractions of numbers

We are going to ...

- use fraction strips to find fractions of quantities and numbers
- find fractions of numbers
- solve simple fraction problems.

You can use a paper strip or 2D shape to help you find a fraction of a number. Finding a fraction is just like division. Sorting the whole into equal groups shows you a fraction of the whole.

denominator
diagram
dividing line
non-unit fraction
numerator
unit fraction

Exercise 12.1

1 A fraction strip is 15 cm long. Majak is marking thirds on the strip.

a Where should he mark $\frac{1}{3}$? At ____ cm.

b Where should he mark $\frac{2}{3}$? At ____ cm.

2 A fraction strip has tenths marked at 5 cm, 10 cm, 15 cm, 20 cm, 25 cm, 30 cm, 35 cm, 40 cm and 45 cm. How long is the whole fraction strip?

3 a Draw a ring around $\frac{1}{10}$ of the marbles.

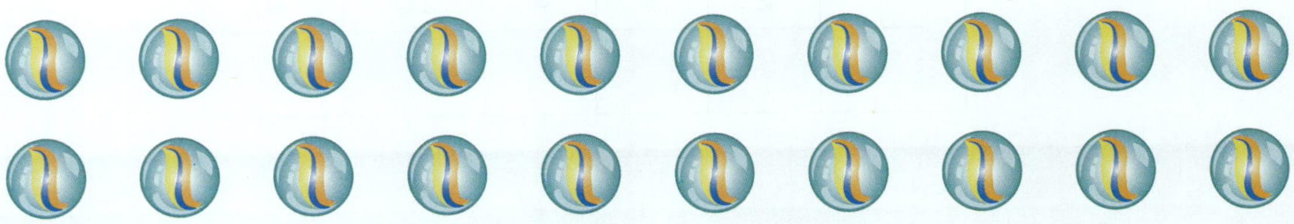

b What fraction of the marbles are not ringed?

4 Here is $\frac{1}{3}$ of a set of cars. How many cars are in the whole set?

5 Find these fractions of 20.

20	$\frac{1}{2}$	$\frac{1}{3}$	$\frac{1}{4}$	$\frac{1}{10}$	$\frac{3}{4}$
		X			

6 In the table below, what is the whole?

	$\frac{1}{2}$	$\frac{1}{3}$	$\frac{1}{4}$	$\frac{1}{10}$	$\frac{3}{4}$
___	X	9	X	X	X

Think like a mathematician

Find a whole number that you can complete the whole table for.

	$\frac{1}{2}$	$\frac{1}{3}$	$\frac{1}{4}$	$\frac{1}{10}$	$\frac{3}{4}$
___					

How did you get started on your investigation?
If you were to carry out the same investigation again, would you do the same thing or would you do something different?

7 Find each fraction and complete the matching division calculation.

a $\frac{1}{4}$ of 8 = ☐, 8 ÷ ☐ = ☐

b $\frac{1}{2}$ of 24 = ☐, 24 ÷ ☐ = ☐

c $\frac{1}{4}$ of 40 = ☐, 40 ÷ ☐ = ☐

8 a Continue the pattern until you reach a quotient of 10.

$\frac{1}{4}$ of 4 = 1, 4 ÷ 4 = 1

$\frac{1}{4}$ of 8 = 2, 8 ÷ 4 = 2

$\frac{1}{4}$ of 12 =

$\frac{1}{4}$ of 16 =

b What do you notice?

____

9 At a party, the sandwiches have been cut into quarters.
Four people share two sandwiches.
How much do they get each?

10 There are four apples in a pack. Roshni takes one apple.
What fraction of the apples does she take?

Arun says that since $\frac{3}{4}$ is three lots of $\frac{1}{4}$, so $\frac{2}{3}$ must be two lots of $\frac{1}{3}$. Do you agree? Why?

Look what I can do!

- ☐ I can use fraction strips to find fractions of quantities and numbers.
- ☐ I can find fractions of numbers.
- ☐ I can solve simple fraction problems.

12.2 Ordering and comparing fractions

We are going to ...

- use a number line from 0 to 1 to order fractions
- compare fractions using a number line or fraction strips, recording using is less than (<) and is greater than (>)
- find fractions that are equivalent in value, recording using the equals sign (=).

You need to know how to order and compare fractions. This will help you to choose the best deal. Would you rather have $\frac{1}{3}$ of \$30 or $\frac{1}{4}$ of \$30?

inequality
multiple

Exercise 12.2

1 Mark $\frac{1}{4}$, $\frac{2}{4}$ and $\frac{3}{4}$ on this number line.

0 ——————————————————————— 1

2 Mark $\frac{1}{3}$, $\frac{2}{3}$ and $\frac{2}{10}$ on this number line.

0 ——————————————————————— 1

3 Which fractions could be marked on a number line between $\frac{3}{4}$ and 1?

4 Use the fraction strips to help you compare $\frac{1}{4}$ and $\frac{1}{5}$.

$\frac{1}{4}$	$\frac{1}{4}$	$\frac{1}{4}$	$\frac{1}{4}$

$\frac{1}{5}$	$\frac{1}{5}$	$\frac{1}{5}$	$\frac{1}{5}$	$\frac{1}{5}$

☐ is less than ☐ ☐ < ☐

☐ is greater than ☐ ☐ > ☐

5 Use <, > or = to complete each statement.

a $\frac{2}{4} \square \frac{1}{2}$

b $\frac{2}{5} \square \frac{1}{5}$

c $\frac{1}{3} \square \frac{2}{3}$

d $\frac{7}{10} \square \frac{9}{10}$

e $\frac{1}{5} \square \frac{1}{10}$

f $\frac{1}{2} \square \frac{1}{3}$

6 Would you rather have $\frac{1}{3}$ or $\frac{1}{4}$ of \$100? Explain why.

____

____

Think like a mathematician

If $\frac{1}{2}$, $\frac{1}{3}$, $\frac{1}{4}$ and $\frac{1}{10}$ of four different whole numbers all have the same value, what can you say about the set of whole numbers? Give some examples.

What did you do to get started on your investigation? If you had to carry out the same investigation again, would you do the same thing or something different?

7 Continue the patterns of the equivalent fractions.

a $\frac{1}{2} = \frac{2}{4} = \frac{\square}{\square} = \frac{\square}{\square} = \frac{\square}{\square} = \frac{\square}{\square}$

b $\frac{1}{10} = \frac{2}{20} = \frac{\square}{\square} = \frac{\square}{\square} = \frac{\square}{\square} = \frac{\square}{\square}$

c $\frac{1}{4} = \frac{\square}{\square} = \frac{\square}{\square} = \frac{\square}{\square} = \frac{\square}{\square}$

Zara says, 'I can see a multiplication table in each set of equivalent fractions!' Explain what Zara means.

8 Draw a diagram to show one of the sets of equivalent fractions in question 7.

Tip

You could draw a fraction wall.

9 Which unit fraction is equivalent to $\frac{9}{27}$? ☐

Look what I can do!

- ☐ I can use a number line from 0 to 1 to order fractions.
- ☐ I can compare fractions using a number line or fraction strips, recording using is less than (<) and is greater than (>).
- ☐ I can find fractions that are equivalent in value, recording using the equals sign (=).

12.3 Calculating with fractions

We are going to ...

- estimate and add fractions with the same denominator (within one whole)
- estimate and subtract fractions with the same denominator (within one whole)
- solve a range of fraction problems.

You can add and subtract fractions because fractions are numbers too. Finding a fraction of a whole has the effect of decreasing the original value.

In a sale, prices are decreased so that you can buy what you wish for less.

decreased
original
reduce

Exercise 12.3

1 What addition is shown on this diagram?
Write the addition number sentence.

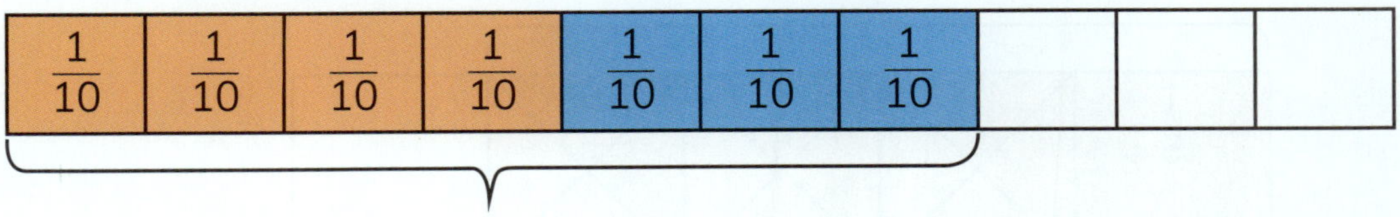

Marcus asked why the answer to question 1 is not $\frac{7}{70}$.
Explain why.

2 Use diagrams or fraction strips to help you complete each addition. Estimate before you calculate.
Draw a ring around your estimate.

a $\frac{1}{3} + \frac{1}{3} =$

estimate: $< \frac{1}{2}$, $= \frac{1}{2}$, $> \frac{1}{2}$

b $\frac{2}{5} + \frac{2}{5} =$

estimate: $< \frac{1}{2}$, $= \frac{1}{2}$, $> \frac{1}{2}$

c $\frac{2}{10} + \frac{3}{10} =$

estimate: $< \frac{1}{2}$, $= \frac{1}{2}$, $> \frac{1}{2}$

d $\frac{1}{2} + \frac{1}{4} =$

estimate: $< \frac{1}{2}$, $= \frac{1}{2}$, $> \frac{1}{2}$

3 Find all the possible solutions for this calculation.

$$\frac{\square}{4} + \frac{\square}{4} = 1$$

Tip

Remember, you can add in any order, so there is no need to record both $\frac{1}{4} + \frac{3}{4} = 1$ and $\frac{3}{4} + \frac{1}{4} = 1$.

4 What subtraction is shown on this diagram?
Write the subtraction number sentence.

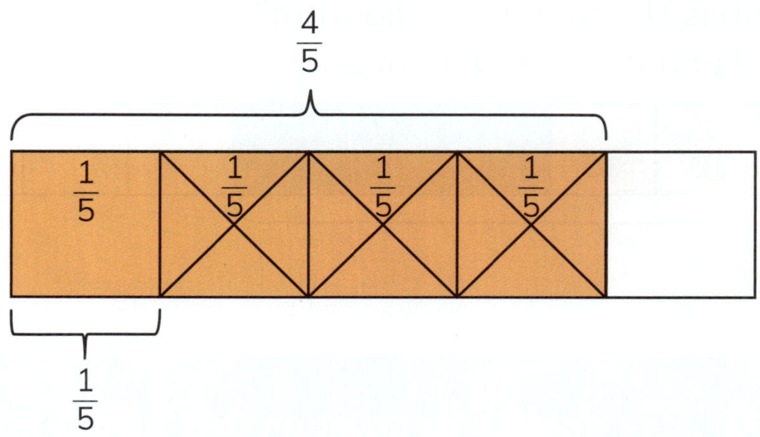

5 Use diagrams or fraction strips to help you complete each subtraction.
Estimate before you calculate. Draw a ring around your estimate.

a $\frac{2}{3} - \frac{2}{3} =$

estimate: $< \frac{1}{2}$, $= \frac{1}{2}$, $> \frac{1}{2}$

b $\frac{3}{5} - \frac{2}{5} =$

estimate: $< \frac{1}{2}$, $= \frac{1}{2}$, $> \frac{1}{2}$

c $1 - \frac{3}{10} =$

estimate: $< \frac{1}{2}$, $= \frac{1}{2}$, $> \frac{1}{2}$

d $1 - \frac{3}{4} =$

estimate: $< \frac{1}{2}$, $= \frac{1}{2}$, $> \frac{1}{2}$

6 Find all the possible solutions for this calculation.

$1 - \frac{\square}{5} = \frac{\square}{5}$

Think like a mathematician

Hien explored adding thirds to make 1 and subtracting thirds from 1. He made this table.

Thirds	
Addition to make 1	**Subtraction from 1**
$\frac{0}{3} + \frac{3}{3} = \frac{3}{3} = 1$	$1 - \frac{3}{3} = \frac{0}{3} = 0$
$\frac{1}{3} + \frac{2}{3} = \frac{3}{3} = 1$	$1 - \frac{2}{3} = \frac{1}{3}$
	$1 - \frac{1}{3} = \frac{2}{3}$
	$1 - \frac{0}{3} = \frac{3}{3} = 1$

Hien says, 'There are twice as many subtractions as there are additions. I wonder if that is true for other fractions too?'
What do you think? Give some examples.

Worked example 1

A clothes shop is having a sale.
The price of a pair of trousers is reduced by $\frac{1}{10}$.

What is the cost of a $30 pair of trousers now?

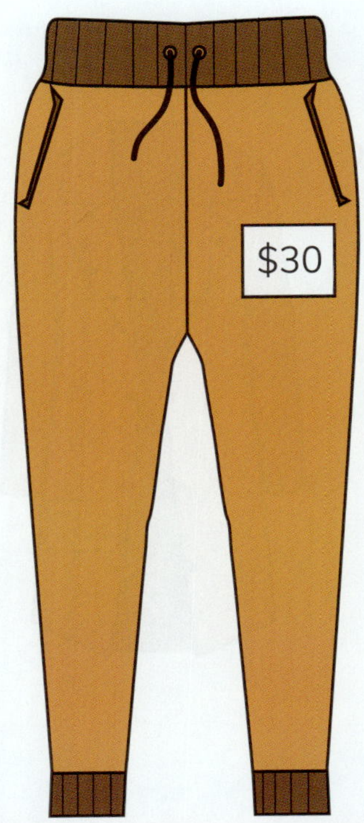

Continued

$\frac{1}{10}$ of 30 = 3

The trousers cost $\frac{1}{10}$ less than they did before the sale.

30 − 3 = 27

The trousers cost $27 now.

I can subtract $\frac{1}{10}$ of the price from the original price to find the reduced price.

7 A clothes shop is having a sale. All prices are reduced by $\frac{1}{4}$.
How much does each item cost now?

a

b

c

d

Look what I can do!

- ☐ I can estimate and add fractions with the same denominator (within one whole).
- ☐ I can estimate and subtract fractions with the same denominator (within one whole).
- ☐ I can solve a range of fraction problems.

Check your progress

1 Put these fractions in order, from smallest to greatest.

$\frac{1}{2}$ $\frac{1}{10}$ $\frac{1}{4}$ $\frac{1}{5}$ $\frac{1}{3}$

2 Use $<$, $>$ or $=$ to complete each statement.

a $\frac{1}{4} \square \frac{1}{3}$

b $\frac{4}{5} \square \frac{2}{5}$

c $\frac{1}{10} \square \frac{1}{5}$

d $\frac{5}{10} \square \frac{1}{2}$

e $\frac{4}{4} \square \frac{10}{10}$

f $\frac{2}{3} \square \frac{3}{3}$

Continued

3 Use diagrams or fraction strips to help you complete each calculation. Estimate before you calculate. Draw a ring around your estimate.

a $\frac{8}{10} - \frac{6}{10} = \square$

estimate: $< \frac{1}{2}$, $= \frac{1}{2}$, $> \frac{1}{2}$

b $\frac{3}{5} + \frac{2}{5} = \square$

estimate: $< \frac{1}{2}$, $= \frac{1}{2}$, $> \frac{1}{2}$

c $\frac{1}{3} + \frac{1}{3} = \square$

estimate: $< \frac{1}{2}$, $= \frac{1}{2}$, $> \frac{1}{2}$

d $1 - \frac{1}{4} = \square$

estimate: $< \frac{1}{2}$, $= \frac{1}{2}$, $> \frac{1}{2}$

Project 4

Dicey fractions

Sofia and Arun are playing a fraction game. They draw a grid like this and write a denominator of 10 in each box:

$\frac{}{10}$	$\frac{}{10}$	$\frac{}{10}$
$\frac{}{10}$	$\frac{}{10}$	$\frac{}{10}$
$\frac{}{10}$	$\frac{}{10}$	$\frac{}{10}$

They take it in turns to roll a 1-6 dice. Every time, they write the number that is rolled as the numerator in one of the boxes.

The winner is the player who makes a line of three boxes that adds up to one whole. (The line of three can be a straight line in any direction.)

Here is a picture of the game after Sofia and Arun have been playing for a little while:

$\frac{1}{10}$	$\frac{3}{10}$	$\frac{}{10}$
$\frac{}{10}$	$\frac{1}{10}$	$\frac{5}{10}$
$\frac{4}{10}$	$\frac{5}{10}$	$\frac{}{10}$

It is Arun's turn. He rolls a 5.

Where do you think Arun should put the 5? Why?

Have a go at playing this game lots of times with a partner.

Do you have any good ways of trying to win?

Does it matter if you go first or second?

13 Measure

Getting started

1 Estimate the mass of four objects in your classroom.

Weigh them.

Use the table below to record what you did.

Share your results with a partner.

Object	Estimated mass	More than 500 grams	Less than 500 grams	Actual mass

This unit will look at three different types of measure: mass, capacity and temperature.

13.1 Mass

We are going to ...

- estimate and measure the mass of objects
- use instruments that measure mass
- use what we know about fractions when describing mass.

gram (g)
kilogram (kg)
mass

Mass is the measure we use when we say that something is heavy or light.

Is an object too heavy to pick up or do you need to use something to lift it?

How much mass is too much for a plane to take off or for a lift to go up and down safely?

Worked example 1

Grandad has 1 kg of rice. He cooks 350 grams of it.

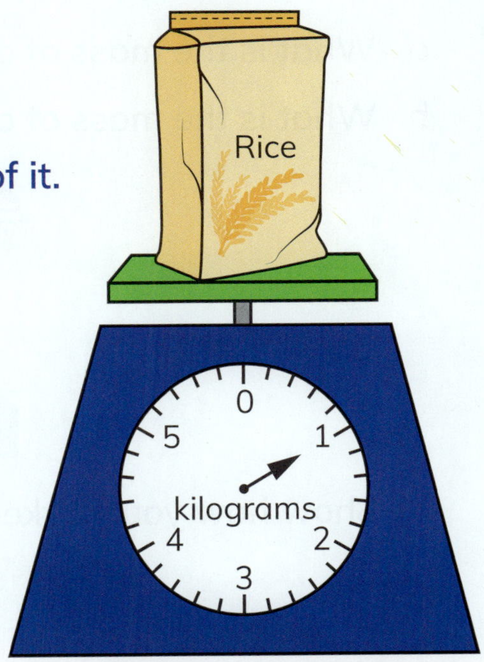

How much rice is left?

1 kilogram is equal to 1000 grams. To find out how much is left change the 1 kg to 1000 grams.

Take 350 g away from 1000 g. This gives 650 g.

When subtracting grams from kilograms, change the kilogram to grams.

Exercise 13.1

1 Suzie buys two peaches and four pears.

One peach weighs 80 grams.

Four pears weigh the same as two peaches.

How much does one pear weigh?

Estimate the mass of four pears before you work it out.

estimate: ________

Show how you worked out the answer.

2 The chocolate bar has a mass of 100 g.

a What is the mass of one muffin?

b What is the mass of each side of the scales?

Show how you worked out the answer.

Is my answer correct?
Could I work it out a different way to check? Try it now.

3 Read the scales.

Write the mass in the boxes below.

Use <, > or = to compare the mass of each pair of objects.

a

b

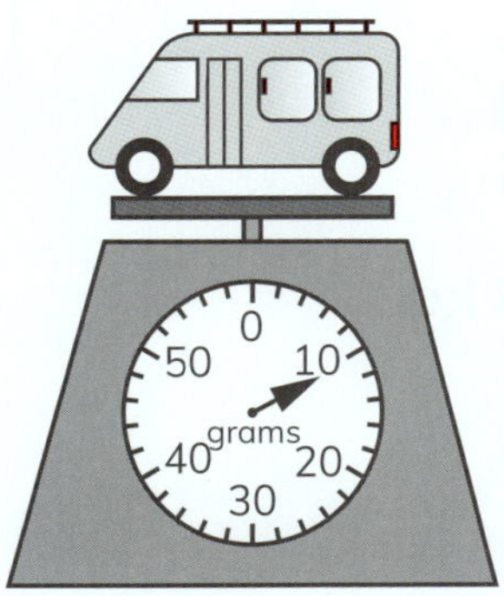

c

4 Draw a circle around your estimate for the mass of each object.

a

8 kg 800 g 80 g

b

7 kg 700 g 70 g

c

5 kg 500 g 5 g

d

4 g 40 g 4 kg

5 You will need a set of scales.

Choose five classroom objects.

Compare the mass of each object by holding two at a time, one in each hand.

Estimate the order of all five from lightest to heaviest.

Write the object names and your estimated mass in order in the table.

Lightest ↑↓ Heaviest

Object	Estimate	Actual mass

Weigh each item separately.

How close were your estimates?

Did you get any surprises?

Did you write the objects in the right order?

6 Choose five different objects that you think have a mass of less than a kilogram.

Hold a kilogram weight in one hand and an object in the other.

Estimate the weight of the object using grams.

Write the name of the object and its estimated mass.

Object	Estimate	Actual mass

Weigh each object and fill in the actual mass column.

How close were your estimates?

Did you get any surprises?

Think like a mathematician

Use these amounts to make each column or row total 1 kg.

200 g 250 g 150 g 300 g 400 g 500 g 450 g 700 g 50 g

Challenge:

Use these amounts to make columns *and* rows that total 1 kg.

500 g 250 g 50 g 450 g 150 g 600 g 250 g 350 g 400 g

How many different ways can the total of 1 kg be found?

Tell a friend how you tried to solve this investigation.

Look what I can do!

- ☐ I can estimate and measure the mass of objects.
- ☐ I can use instruments that measure mass.

13.2 Capacity

We are going to ...

- estimate and measure capacity in millilitres and litres
- use instruments that measure capacity.

capacity
litres (L)
millilitres (ml)

Capacity is the total amount that something can hold.

A teaspoon holds 5 millilitres.

It can be used to measure how much medicine you need to take.

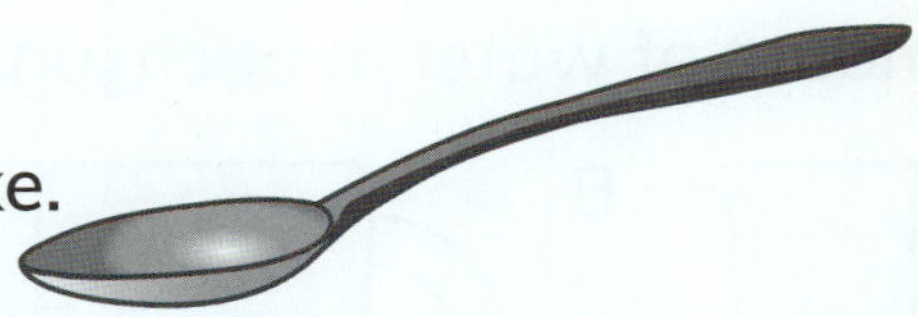

This bottle can hold half a litre.

If the bottle is not full, you will have less than half a litre.

Your bowl can hold a quarter of a litre.

If you fill it with cereal and add milk, then the amount of milk will be less than a quarter of a litre.

Worked example 2

These containers use different scales. Jug 1 is marked in millilitres and jug 2 is marked in litres.

Which jug has the most water?

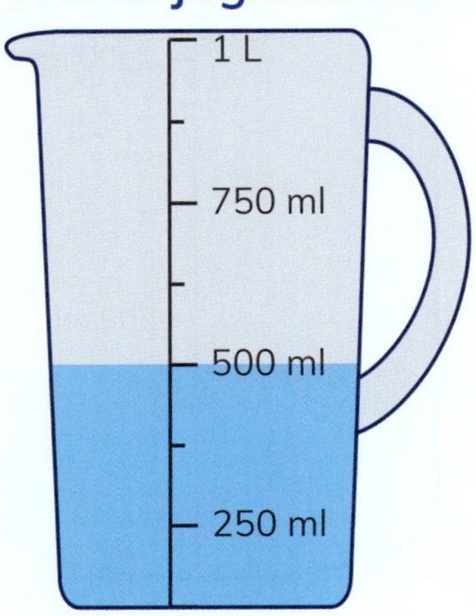

jug 1

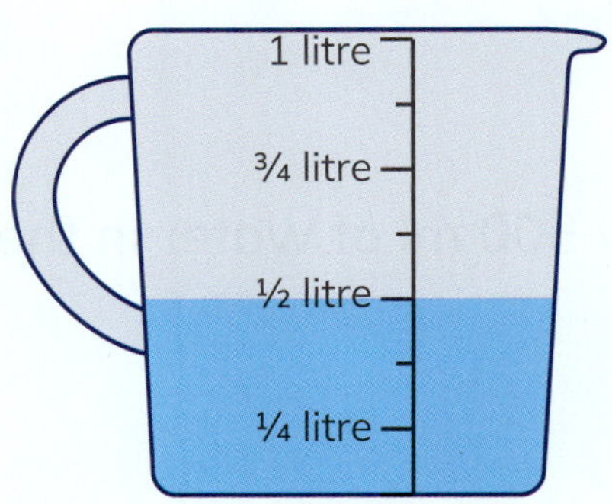

jug 2

Continued

Jug 1 has the capacity of 1 litre but it is filled to 500 ml.

Jug 2 has the capacity to hold 1 litre and it is filled to $\frac{1}{2}$ litre.

Both jugs have the same amount of water because 500 ml = $\frac{1}{2}$ litre.

Exercise 13.2

1 Each jug has a capacity of 1 litre.

a Record the amount of water in each jug.

A
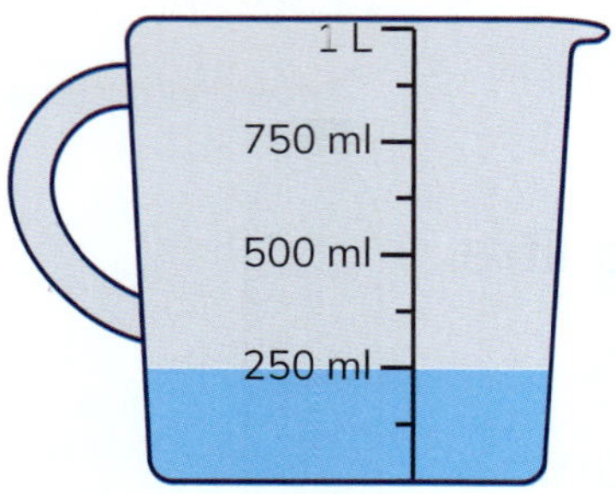

B
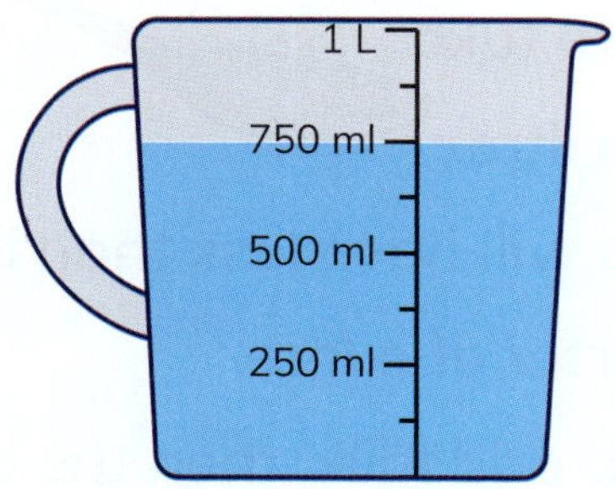

C
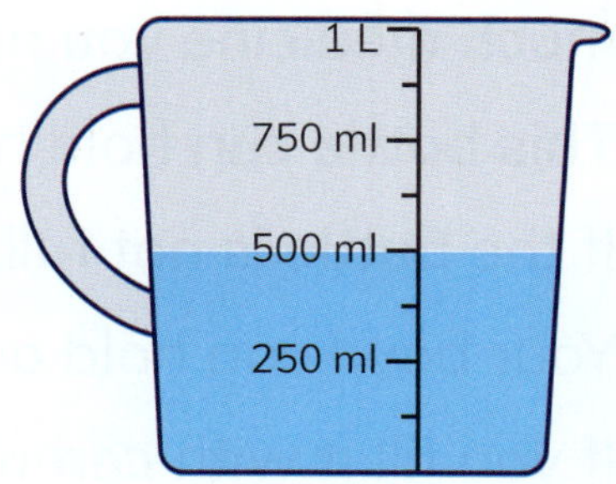

__________ __________ __________

b Put the containers in order from the largest amount of water to the smallest.

____

c Look at this jug. Is the capacity larger, smaller or the same as one of the jugs above? How do you know?.

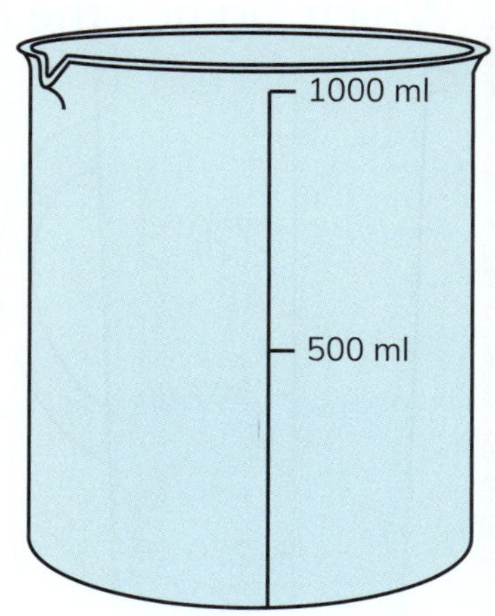

____

d Use a ruler to draw 500 ml of water in the jug.

____

2 Label each set with the total amount of drink.
Each tin has a capacity of 250 ml.

a

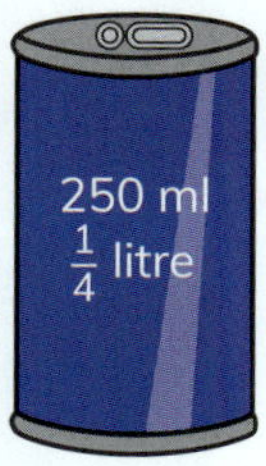

________ ml

________ litre

b

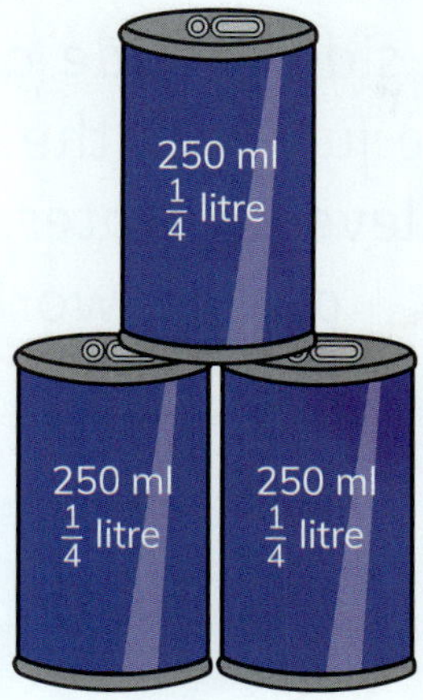

________ ml

________ litre

c

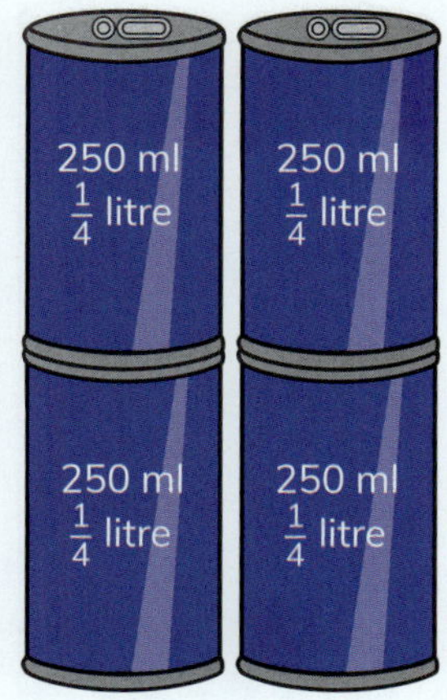

________ ml

________ litre

Four cans hold 1 litre. How many litres are in each of these boxes?

d

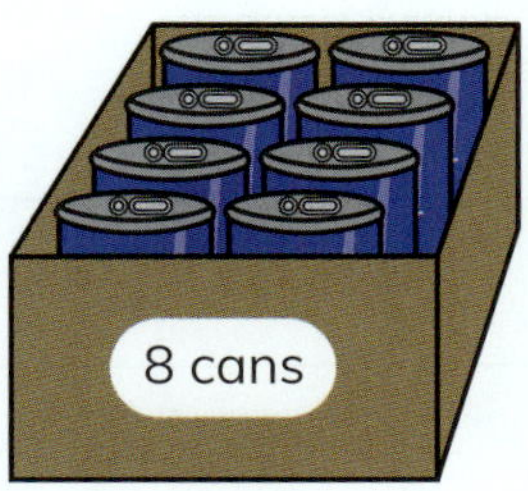

________ litres

e

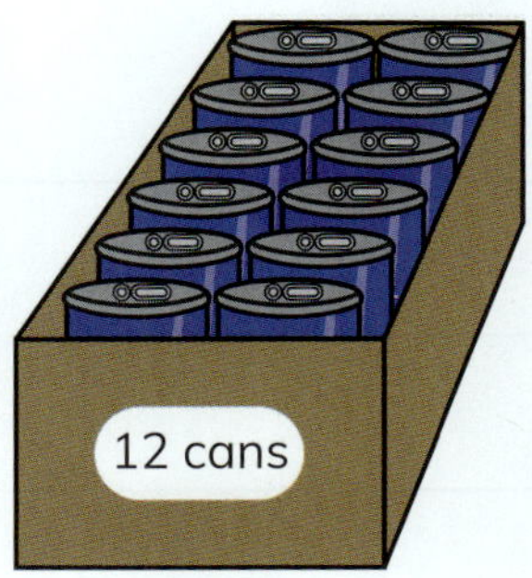

________ litres

f

________ litres

3

Is Marcus correct?

Explain your answer.

4 Each jug has the capacity to hold 1000 ml of liquid.

Use what you know to estimate these measurements.
Then round each value to the nearest marked division.

a

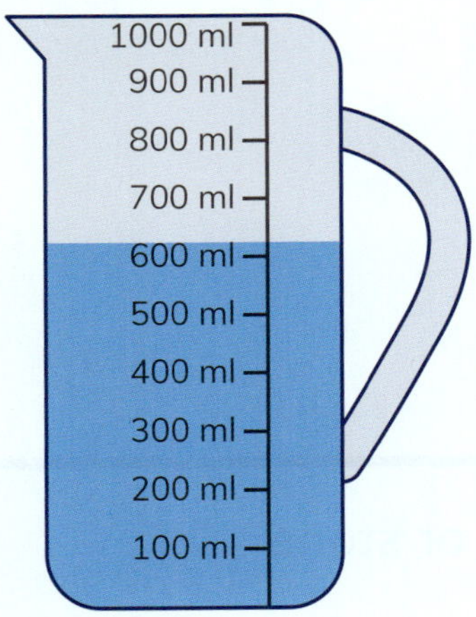

Estimate: __________

Rounded to: __________

b

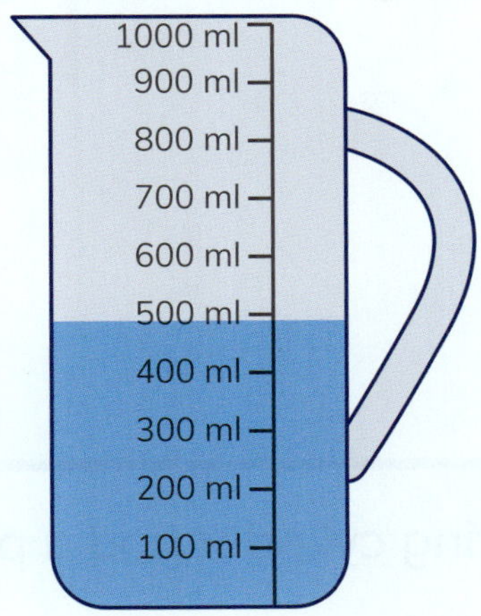

Estimate: __________

Rounded to: __________

c

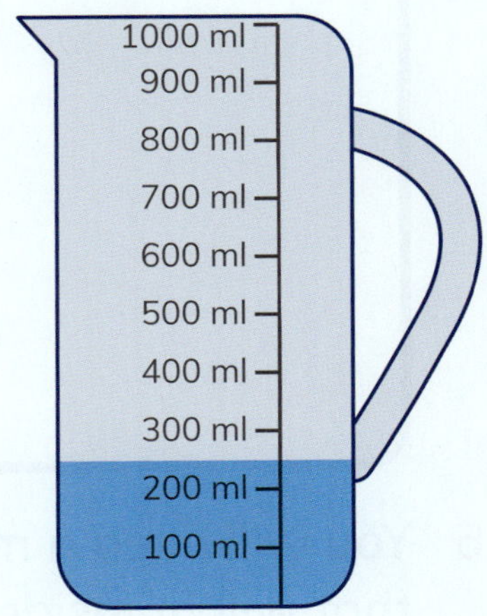

Estimate: __________

Rounded to: __________

5 Use a container that can hold water.

Estimate the level of a litre. Mark it on the container.

Check your estimate by pouring a litre of water into your container.

How close was your estimate?

____

Now estimate the level of 2 litres. Mark it on the container.

Check your estimate by pouring in another litre of water into your container.

How close was your estimate?

____

Draw three containers. One empty, one showing a litre full and one showing 2 litres full.

Mark the scale on the bottle.

Write where you think 3 litres would be.

6 You will need a measuring cylinder and a pebble or stone that will fit inside it.

Fill a measuring cylinder to about half full.

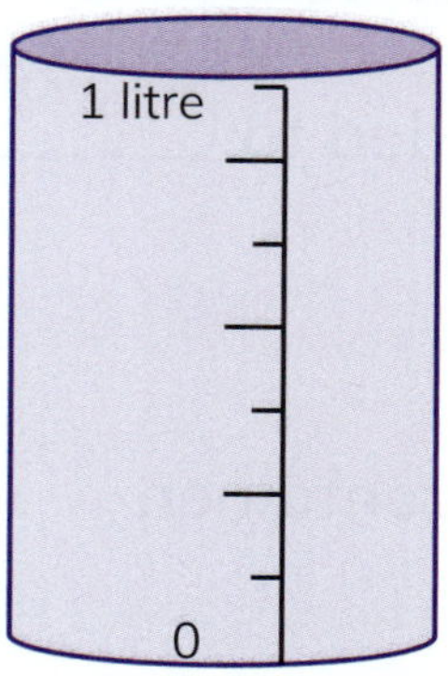

Record the water level at the start in the table.

Slowly add a large pebble into the water.

What happens to the water level?

Complete the table.

Level of water at the start	
New level with the stone	
Difference	

Think like a mathematician

Work with a partner.

Cup A holds 500 millilitres.

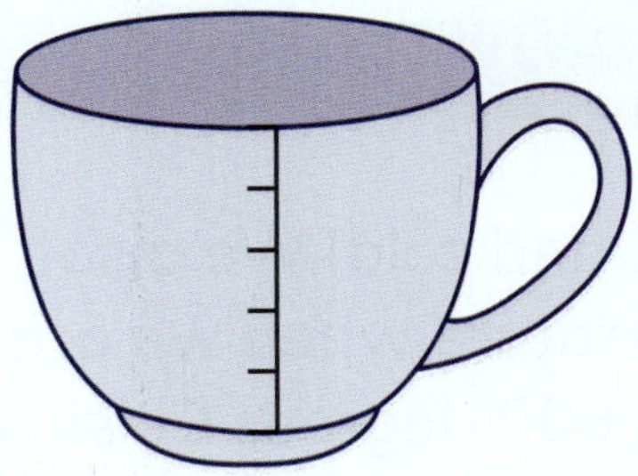

Cup B holds 300 millilitres.

Tip

You can pour one cup into the other.

Using only full cups, show how you can make

a 1000 millilitres

b 700 millilitres

c 100 millilitres

d Could you use the two cups to make all the different hundreds of millilitres from 100 to 1000?

Did you predict the answer before you started investigating?

Look what I can do!

- [ ] I can estimate and measure capacity in millilitres and litres.
- [ ] I can use instruments that measure capacity.

13.3 Temperature

We are going to ...

- use instruments that measure temperature
- read the scales on a thermometer.

degrees Celsius (°C)

Everyone knows about hot and cold. We also need to know about temperature when we are cooking. Bake a chicken at 600 degrees Celsius and the chicken would burn very quickly!

Putting a teabag into a mug of cold water would not work.

If the temperature outside goes up or down, then you will need to change your clothes.

Worked example 3

a Read the scale. Write the temperature.

A

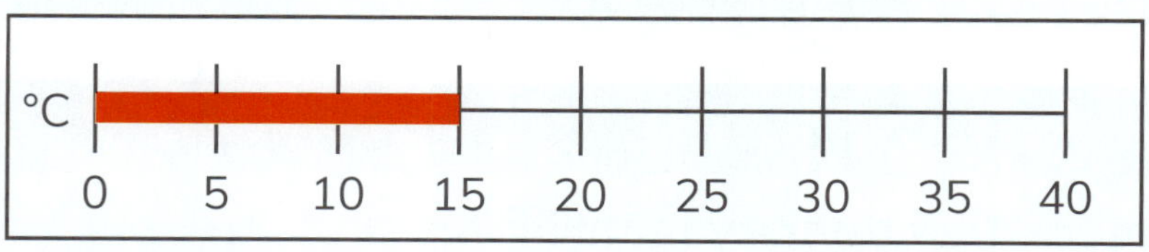

B

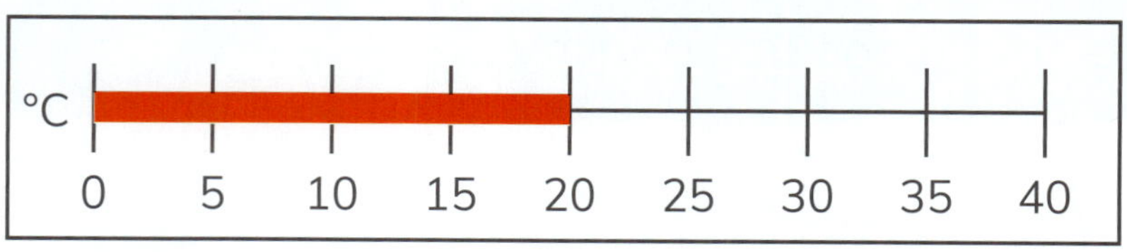

b Which shows the higher temperature, thermometer A or thermometer B?

c Draw a line to show a temperature of 25 °C.

Continued

a Thermometer A is 15 °C.

Thermometer B is 20 °C.

b The red line shows the temperature on each thermometer. The longer the line, the hotter it is. Thermometer B shows the higher temperature.

c

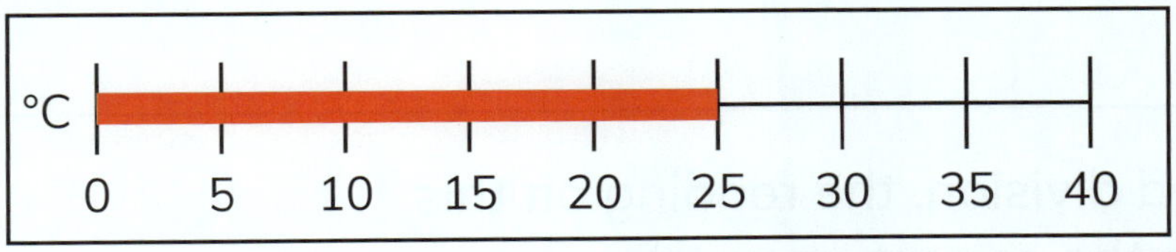

Exercise 13.3

1 Write the temperatures shown on the thermometers.
Round each temperature to the nearest 10 °C.

a

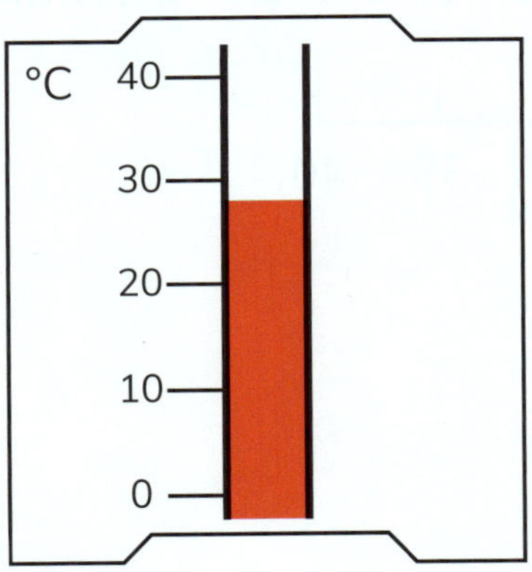

b

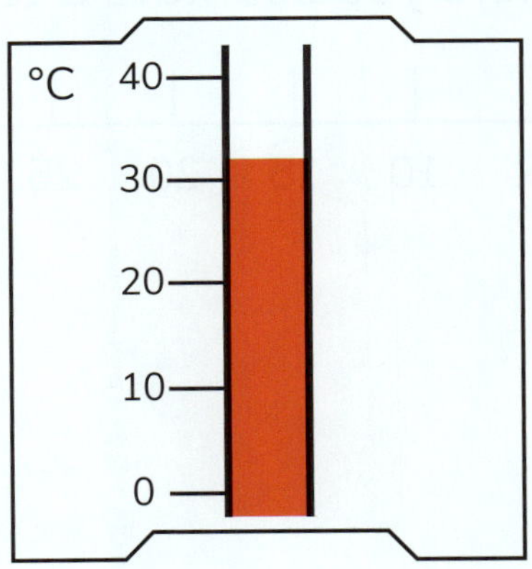

c

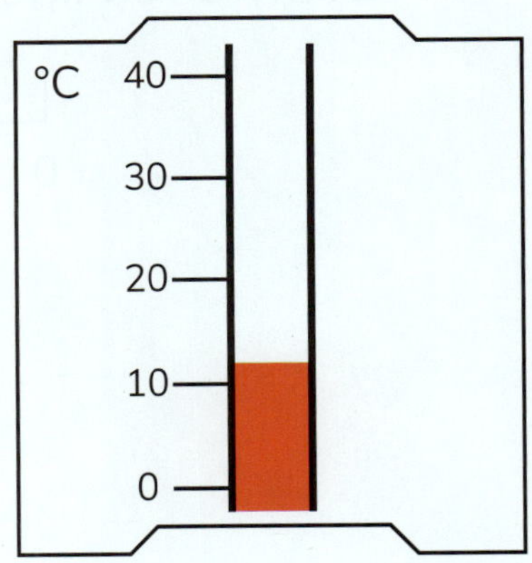

2 Marianna reads the thermometer to the nearest division. Her answer is 20 °C.

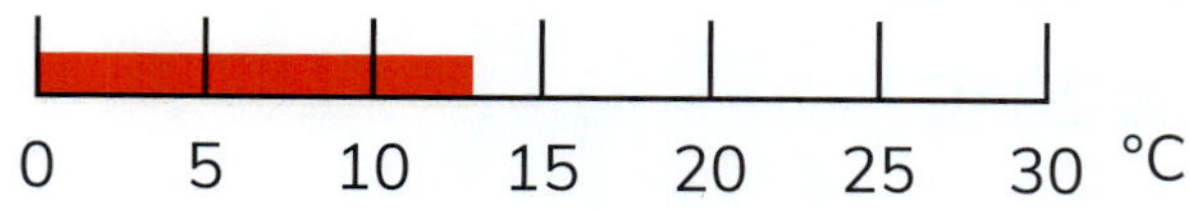

a Is Marianna right? If she is not right, what should the answer be?

____

b To the nearest marked division, the reading on this thermometer is (circle the correct answer):

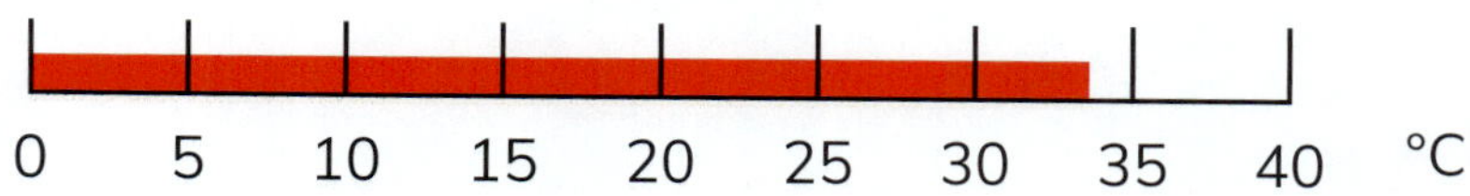

25 °C 30 °C 35 °C

c Draw a red line where you estimate a temperature of 27 °C would be.

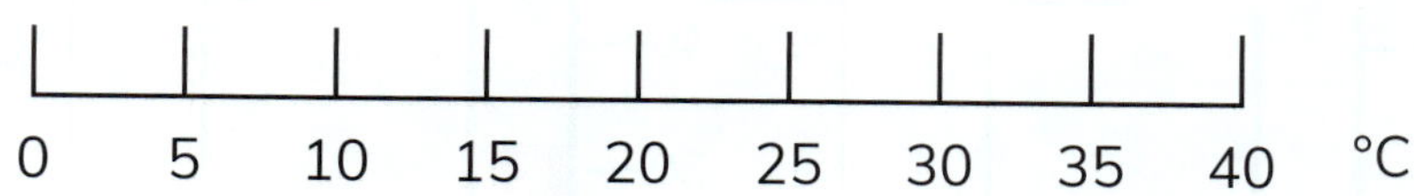

3

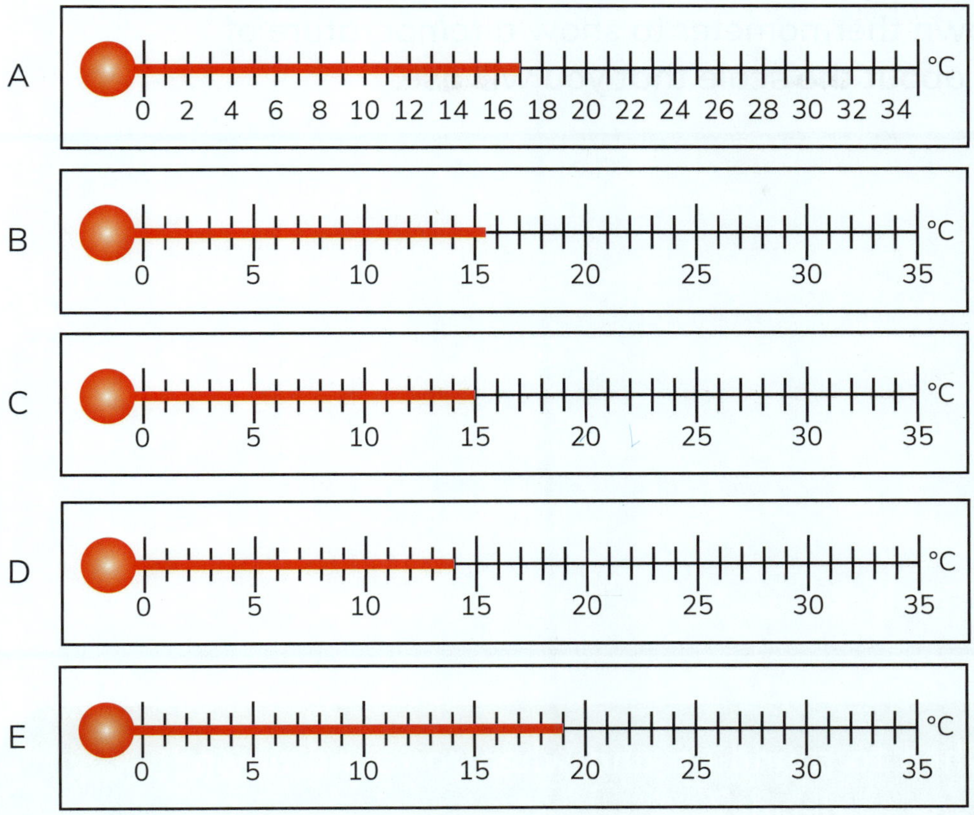

a Which thermometers have labelled intervals of 5 °C?

____

b To the nearest labelled division, what temperature does thermometer A show?

____

c To the nearest labelled division, what temperature does thermometer B show?

____

d Look at thermometers C and D. Which shows the higher temperature?

____

e To the nearest labelled division, what temperature does thermometer E show?

____

f Draw your own thermometer to show a temperature of 26 °C. Think about the scale that you will use.

How do I know when to round up and when to round down? What would help me to decide?

4 Work as a group of four.

You will each need your own thermometer.

You will be taking and recording temperatures around the school.

Decide on four different locations. Place 1 thermometer in each location.

Leave them there for 10 minutes.

Meanwhile, list your locations in the table and write down your estimated temperatures. Discuss your answers as a group.

Location	Estimated temperature	Actual temperature

When 10 minutes have passed, collect your thermometers and record the actual temperatures in your table.

Now complete these sentences.

The temperature in the ____________ is ____________ .

The ____________ is ____________ than the ____________ .

The difference in temperature between the ____________ and the ____________ is ________ degrees Celsius.

Write three more sentences of your own telling and comparing temperatures.

1 ____

2 ____

3 ____

5 Work with a partner.

You will each need a thermometer and a waterproof container.

Fill one container with wet soil. Fill the other with dry sand.

Place a thermometer in each of the containers.

Container	Estimated temperature	Actual temperature after 30 minutes
Wet soil		
Dry sand		

Discuss with your partner the estimated temperature of both containers after 30 minutes and record your estimates in the table.

Now check the thermometers.

Is it what you thought?

Describe what happened and why you think the temperatures were the same or different.

____

____

Think like a mathematician

Design a poster that shows what you know about temperature.
Use pictures, words and thermometers.
Use the words 'degrees', 'Celsius' and 'temperature'.

Have I shown on my poster all that I know?
What else can I put on my poster? Make at least one improvement.

Look what I can do!

☐ I can use instruments that measure temperature.

☐ I can read the scales on a thermometer.

Check your progress

1 To the nearest labelled division, write the mass shown on each scale.

a

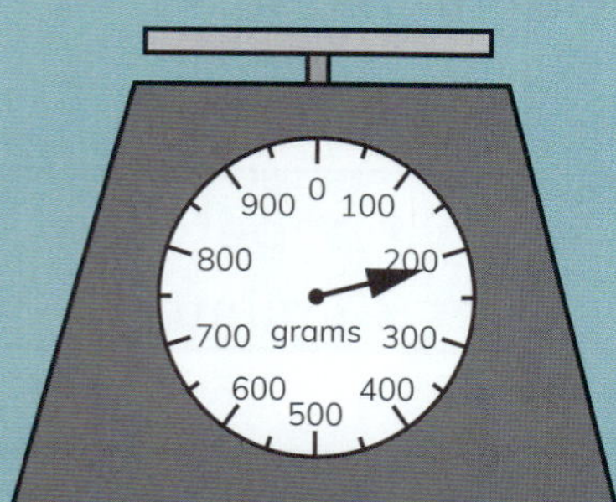

Estimate: ______

b

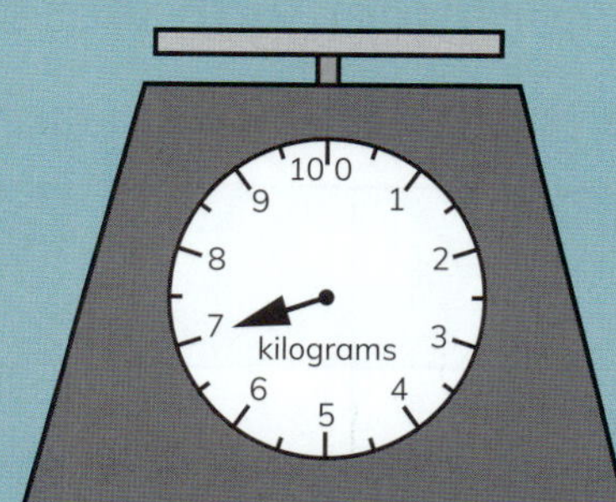

Estimate: ______

c

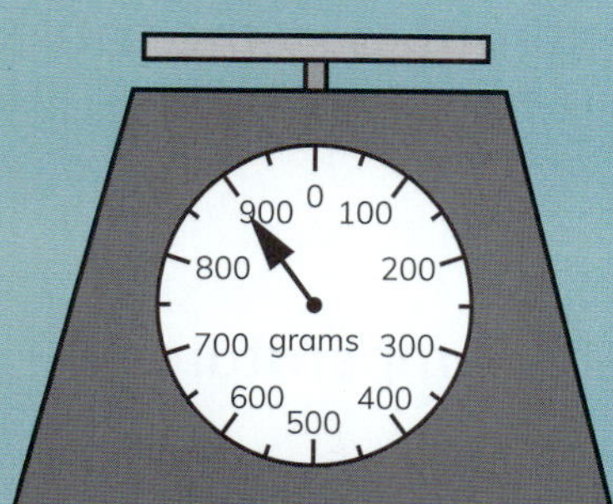

Estimate: ______

d

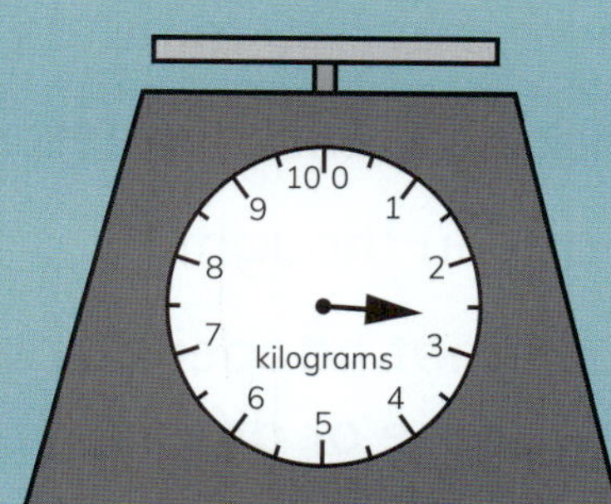

Estimate: ______

Continued

2 To the nearest labelled division, write how much liquid is in these containers.

a

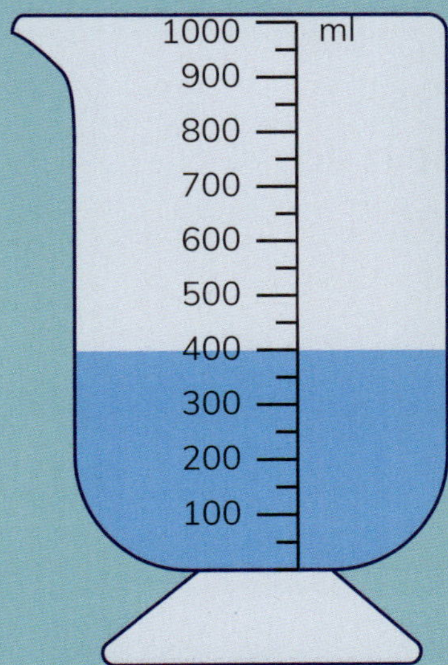

______

b

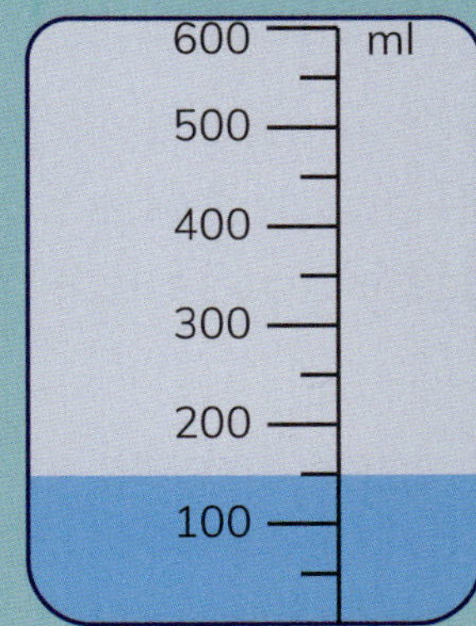

______

c Draw two containers with water.
Show one quarter of a litre in one container and 350 ml in the other.
Which container has the most?

Continued

3 a If a plum weighs about 50 grams, how much would eight plums weigh?

____

b Chiwitel's medicine bottle holds 55 millilitres.
Chiwitel has to take 5 millilitres of medicine a day.
How many days until the medicine is finished?

____

c Aisha's snail crawls 48 cm. Erik's snail crawls 72 cm.
How much farther than Aisha's snail does Erik's snail crawl?

____

4 This morning the temperature outside was 18 °C.
It went up by 7 °C by 3 o'clock and then it went down 1 °C per hour until midnight.
What is the temperature at midnight?

____

14 Time (2)

Getting started

1 Write the times below each clock.

a

____

b

____

c

____

d

____

2 Write the times from question 1 on these digital clocks.

a [:]   b [:]   c [:]   d [:]

Continued

3 Draw the hands on these clocks to show the times.

a 

5:55

b 

1:34

c 

6:17

d 

9:12

You often need to measure time. For example, when you are:

- running a race
- meeting friends
- catching a bus or a train
- baking your favourite cake.

14.1 Time

We are going to ...

- choose units of time for activities
- learn about time intervals.

We all have the same amount of time, but we use it in different ways.

Time is measured in minutes, hours, days, weeks, months and years.

How will you use your time today?

time

time interval

Exercise 14.1

1 Estimate how many times you can do these in 1 minute.

a Walk around your classroom. ________

b Stand up and sit down. ________

c Estimate how long you can stand on one leg without wobbling. ________

Try it. How close was your estimate?

____

e What happens at home or at school that takes about an hour to do?

____

f What would you do that lasts about a day?

____

g What could you do that lasts a week?

____

2 Use the calendar to find the answers.

January						
M	T	W	T	F	S	S
				1	2	3
4	5	6	7	8	9	10
11	12	13	14	15	16	17
18	19	20	21	22	23	24
25	26	27	28	29	30	31

February						
M	T	W	T	F	S	S
1	2	3	4	5	6	7
8	9	10	11	12	13	14
15	16	17	18	19	20	21
22	23	24	25	26	27	28

March						
M	T	W	T	F	S	S
1	2	3	4	5	6	7
8	9	10	11	12	13	14
15	16	17	18	19	20	21
22	23	24	25	26	27	28
29	30	31				

a How many days are **between** 22nd January and 18th February?

____

Tip

The question asks how many days are **between** the two dates, so you do not need to count the two dates themselves.

b What is the date three weeks after 1st March?

____

c Carnival day is 17th March. Plans are made six weeks before that. What date do they start planning?

____

d Zalika plans a holiday to last three weeks. She leaves on 19th January. When does she arrive back?

____

3 a Many airlines ask you to buy a ticket 14 days before your flight. If Thandiwe leaves on 20th June, on what day should he buy his ticket?

____

b Misha arrives at the hotel on 8th July and will stay three nights. What date will Misha check out of the hotel?

____

c Abida turns seven years old on 11th September. Jim turns seven years old on 18th September. How many days older is Abida?

____

d Stefania will be 13 years old on 7th October 2023.
In what year was she born?
How old will she be on 7th October 2030?

____

What would have helped you to work out the answers?

4 a How many days are there between
3rd June 2022 and 25th November 2022?

____

Tip

The question asks how many days are **between** the two dates, so you do not need to count the two dates themselves.

June

M	T	W	T	F	S	S
		1	2	3	4	5
6	7	8	9	10	11	12
13	14	15	16	17	18	19
20	21	22	23	24	25	26
27	28	29	30			

July

M	T	W	T	F	S	S
				1	2	3
4	5	6	7	8	9	10
11	12	13	14	15	16	17
18	19	20	21	22	23	24
25	26	27	28	29	30	31

August

M	T	W	T	F	S	S
1	2	3	4	5	6	7
8	9	10	11	12	13	14
15	16	17	18	19	20	21
22	23	24	25	26	27	28
29	30	31				

September

M	T	W	T	F	S	S
			1	2	3	4
5	6	7	8	9	10	11
12	13	14	15	16	17	18
19	20	21	22	23	24	25
26	27	28	29	30		

October

M	T	W	T	F	S	S
					1	2
3	4	5	6	7	8	9
10	11	12	13	14	15	16
17	18	19	20	21	22	23
24	25	26	27	28	29	30
31						

November

M	T	W	T	F	S	S
	1	2	3	4	5	6
7	8	9	10	11	12	13
14	15	16	17	18	19	20
21	22	23	24	25	26	27
28	29	30				

b Daniel was born on 10th January 2003.
How old will he be on his birthday in 2018?

____

c Lily's holiday is from 9th May to 21st May.
Song's holiday starts on 12th May and lasts two weeks.
Whose holiday is longer and by how many days?

____

5 Solve the calendar questions.

April						
M	T	W	T	F	S	S
	1	2	3	4	5	6
7	8	9	10	11	12	13
14	15	16	17	18	19	20
21	22	23	24	25	26	27
28	29	30				

a I packed a suitcase on 7th April to visit my grandma in three days' time. I will stay for nine days.

What day and date will I get home?

____

b My friend was coming to stay on 16th April for three days. She was ill and couldn't come for another week. Then she stayed for 5 days.

What day and date did she go home?

____

6 Only children aged 10 and above can ride the rollercoaster.
Nabil is eight years old and Gina is nine years old.
How many years do they have to wait until they can both ride the rollercoaster together?

____

7 What can you measure using different units of time?

Write two examples for each.

Years __________ __________

Months __________ __________

Days __________ __________

Hours __________ __________

Minutes __________ __________

Think like a mathematician

Work with a partner.

You will need a minute timer.

Take turns to walk the length of a space or around your playground for 1 minute.

Count how many steps you took.

How many steps did you each walk in a minute?

____

If you walked for 2 minutes, do you think that you would walk twice the number of steps? Explain your thinking.

____

____

How many steps could you walk in 10 minutes? In 30 minutes? In an hour?

____

Would the walk get slower if it was for an hour?

Look what I can do!

- [ ] I can choose units of time for activities.
- [ ] I can work out time intervals.

14.2 Timetables

We are going to ...

- read and use the information in timetables.

Timetables are very useful when you wish to plan a journey, go on a holiday or meet your friends if you travel by bus, train or plane.

timetable

Timetables tell you when the bus, train or plane leaves and when it arrives.

Timetables also tell you what is happening in your days at school.

Worked example 1

This timetable shows a day at school.

Maths	Science	Art	Music	Games	Literacy
9 – 10 a.m.	10 – 10.45 a.m.	11 – 11.30 a.m.	12 – 12.30 p.m.	1 – 2.15 p.m.	2.30 – 3.15 p.m.

a What time does the art lesson start?

b What time does the music lesson end?

Worked example 1

a Art starts at 11 in the morning.

b Music ends at 12.30 in the afternoon.

Find the lesson in the table. This shows the start and finish times for the lesson.

Exercise 14.2

1 Use the timetable to answer the questions.

Bus stop	Bus 1	Bus 2	Bus 3	Bus 4
Orange Street	7:40	7:55	8:15	8:30
Baker Avenue	7:54	8:09	8:32	–
School	8:22	8:19	8:45	–
Genesta Road	8:46	8:43	8:59	9:10
Altash Way	9:02	8:50	–	–

a What time does Bus 2 arrive at Altash Way?

____

b Sara lives at Orange Street. She gets the bus at 8:15. What time does she arrive at school?

____

c Razaan lives at Baker Avenue. He needs to get to school by 8.30. What buses could he catch to arrive in time?

____

d Razaan is travelling home from school. He says that this timetable is not helpful. Is he correct? Explain your answer.

____

2 Here is part of a train timetable.

Destination	Train 1	Train 2	Train 3	Train 4	Train 5	Train 6
Brightville	8:01	9:26	10:43	11.17	1:18	2:36
Blue City	8:23	9:38	10:58	11:25	1:30	2:46
Central Town	8:31	–		11:38	–	2:58
Downton	8:37	–	11.23	11:51	1:58	–

a A train leaves Brightville at 10:43.
What time does it arrive at Downton?

____

b A train leaves Blue City at 2:46.
What time does it get to Central Town?

____

c Which trains do not stop at Downton?

____

d What time does the train leave from Blue City to get to Central Town at 11:38?

____

e What time does the train leave from Brightsville to arrive at Central Town at 8:31?

____

Think like a mathematician

You are going to make your own timetable. You can use the empty timetable below or you can draw your own on a separate piece of paper.

a First think about what lessons you have today. Write these into the heading boxes.

b Write down when each lesson begins and when it ends.

c Ask a partner questions about your timetable. For example, what time does a lesson start?

d Draw your perfect timetable.

Think about your favourite lessons. Would you have them more than once?

Look what I can do!

☐ I can read and use the information in timetables.

Check your progress

1 a How many months are there between 25th January 2026 and 25th March 2026?

____

b How many days are there between 25th January 2026 and 25th February 2026? ________

c How many weeks are there between 11th February 2026 and 25th February 2026? ________

January 2026

M	T	W	T	F	S	S
			1	2	3	4
5	6	7	8	9	10	11
12	13	14	15	16	17	18
19	20	21	22	23	24	25
26	27	28	29	30	31	

February 2026

M	T	W	T	F	S	S
						1
2	3	4	5	6	7	8
9	10	11	12	13	14	15
16	17	18	19	20	21	22
23	24	25	26	27	28	

March 2026

M	T	W	T	F	S	S
						1
2	3	4	5	6	7	8
9	10	11	12	13	14	15
16	17	18	19	20	21	22
23	24	25	26	27	28	29
30	31					

2 This timetable shows activities for a week at holiday camp.

	Monday	Tuesday	Wednesday	Thursday	Friday
10:00	Walk	Reading	Reading	Walk	Walk
11:00	Swimming	Swimming	Swimming	Reading	Swimming
12:00	Lunch	Lunch	Walk	Lunch	Lunch
1:00	Football	Walk	Lunch	Singing	Bike ride
2:00	Tennis	Games	Tennis	Tennis	Tennis

a What day is there a late lunch? ________

b What day is singing? ________

c What time does singing start? ________

d What day do the children not need a tennis racquet? ________

Continued

3

Train timetable				
	First train	Second train	Third train	Fourth train
Blueberry Hill	7:30	8:05	8:25	9:20
Sunny Meadow	7:47	–	8:42	9:39
Redwood Place	8:00	8:40	8:59	10:00

a Grandma wants to go to Sunny Meadow from Blueberry Hill. What time does the earliest train leave the station?

____

b Grandad missed the earliest train from Sunny Meadow to Redwood Place. What time is the next train?

____

c Aman wants to go to Sunny Meadow. She does not mind what time she arrives. Which train can she not go on?

____

15 Angles and movement

Getting started

1 An angle is the amount of turn between two lines that meet each other at a single point.

Draw the line that shows:

a a quarter turn clockwise

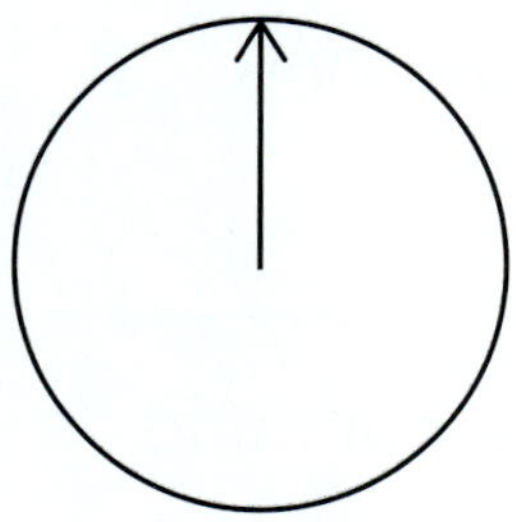

b a quarter turn anticlockwise

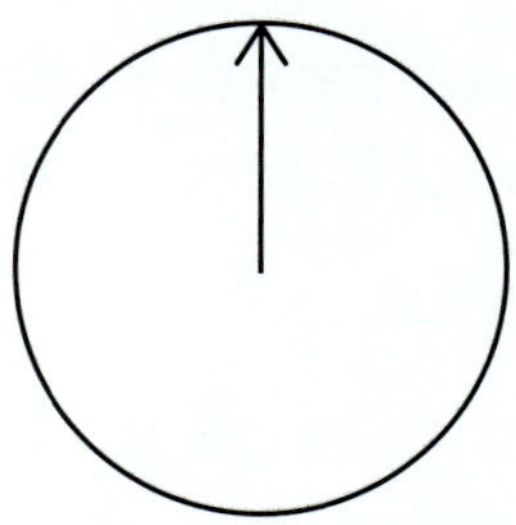

c a half turn clockwise

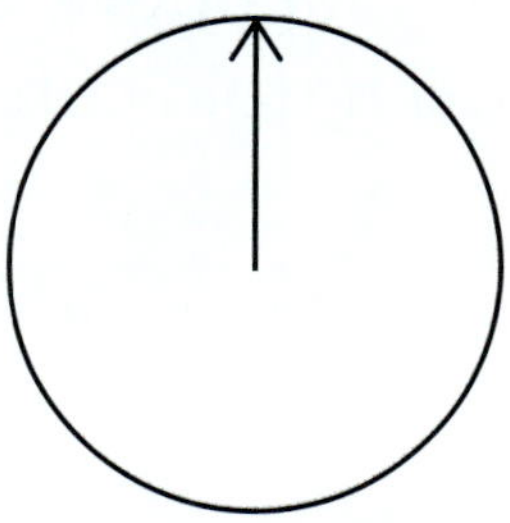

d a half turn anticlockwise.

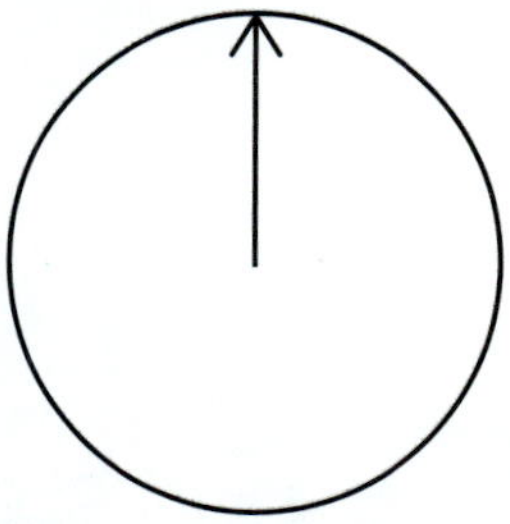

2 For each line that you drew in question 1, write one thing that you notice about it.

____

____

An angle is an amount of turn.

Knowing about north, south, east and west can help us to find our way or give directions.

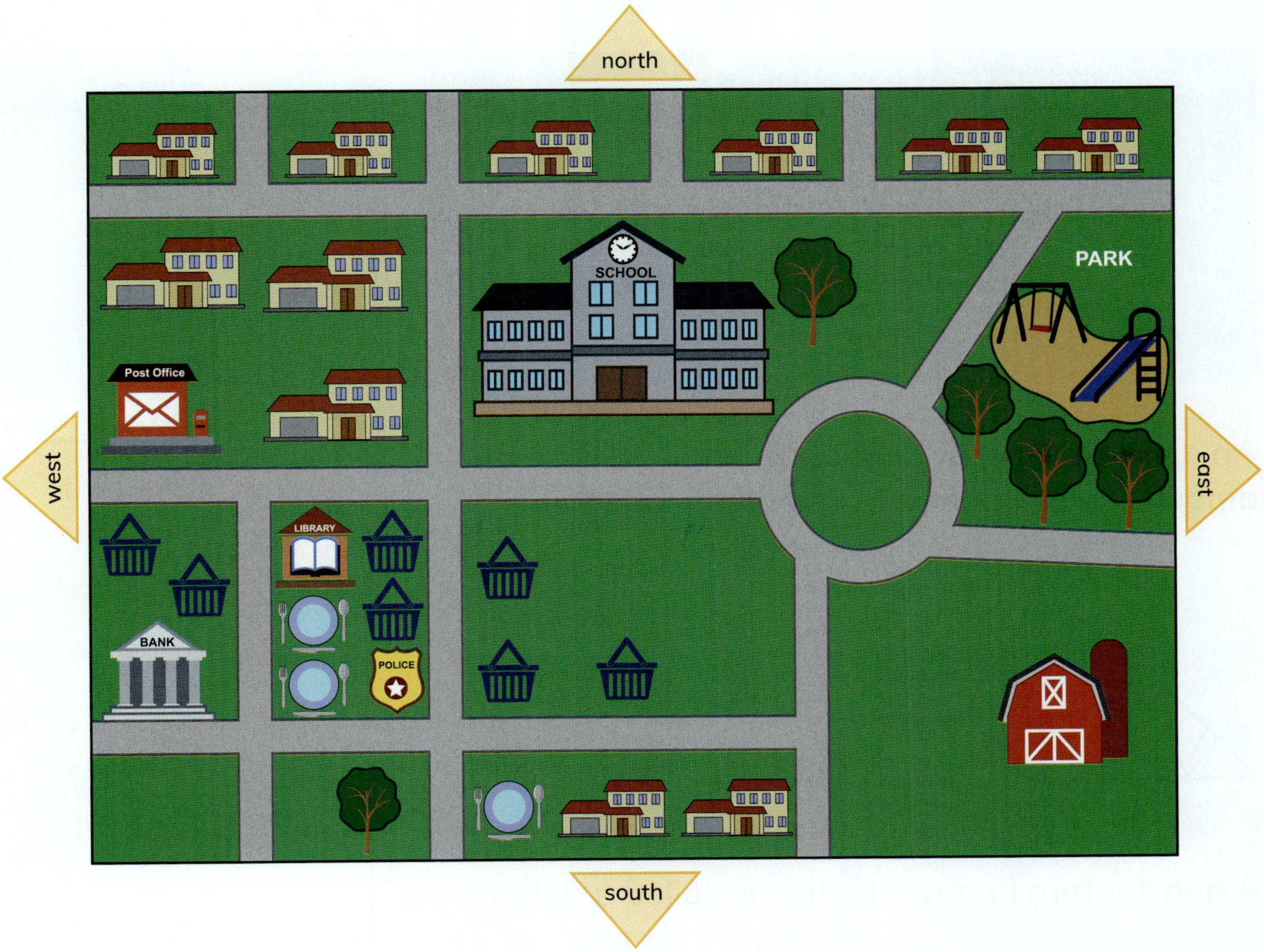

15.1 Angles, direction, position and movement

We are going to ...

- compare angles
- learn about north, south, east and west
- use words to describe position, direction and movement
- make simple grid maps.

An angle is a measurement of turn. It tells us the amount of turn from one position to another.

cardinal points
compass
right angle

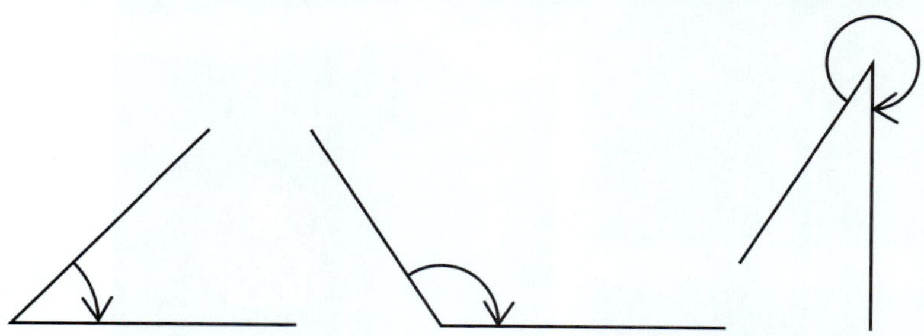

A quarter turn in any direction is called a right angle.

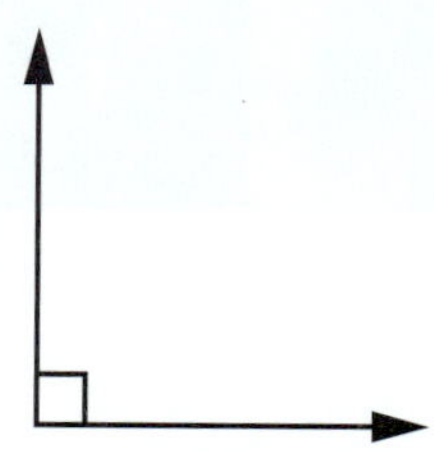

Two right angles together make a straight line.

This is also a half turn.

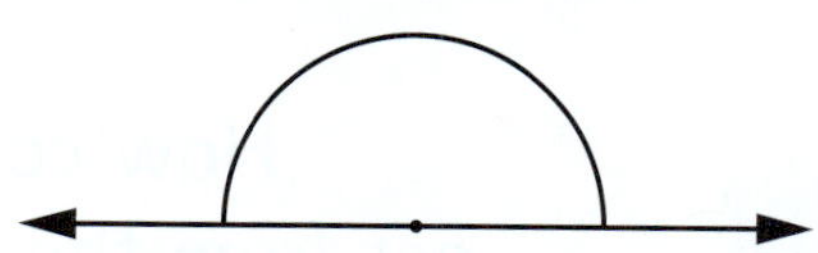

Two half turns in the same direction make a complete circle, or a full turn.

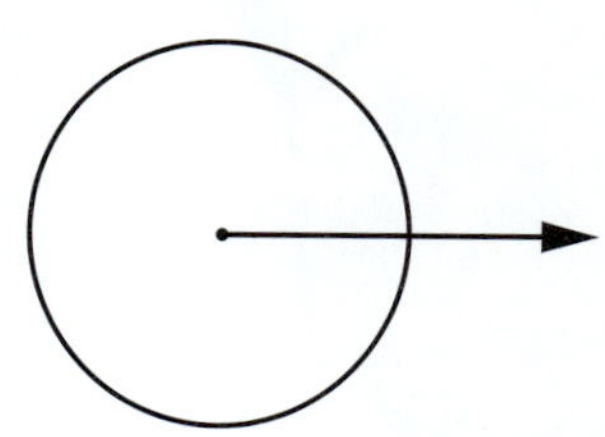

Exercise 15.1

1 We are going to make a right angle measure.

Take a piece of paper.

Fold it in half vertically.

Fold it in half again horizontally.

You have made a right angle.

a Find right angles in your classroom using your right angle measure. Look at your table, your book or a window.

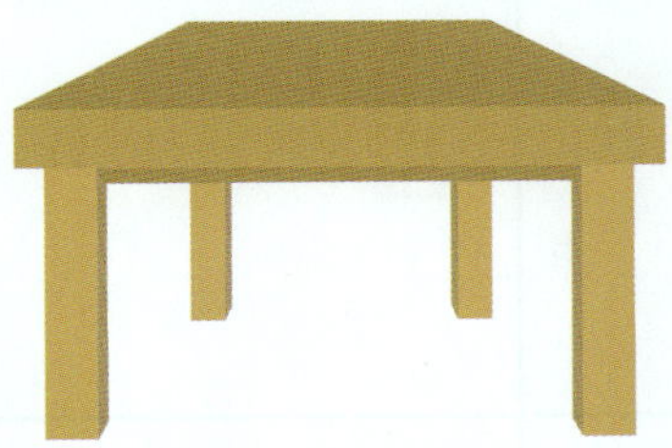

b Draw what you find. Mark the angle.

2 Use your right angle measure to find in your classroom:

- four right angles
- four angles that are greater than a right angle
- four angles that are less than a right angle.

Write and draw the angles that you found.

Right angle	Greater than a right angle	Less than a right angle

3

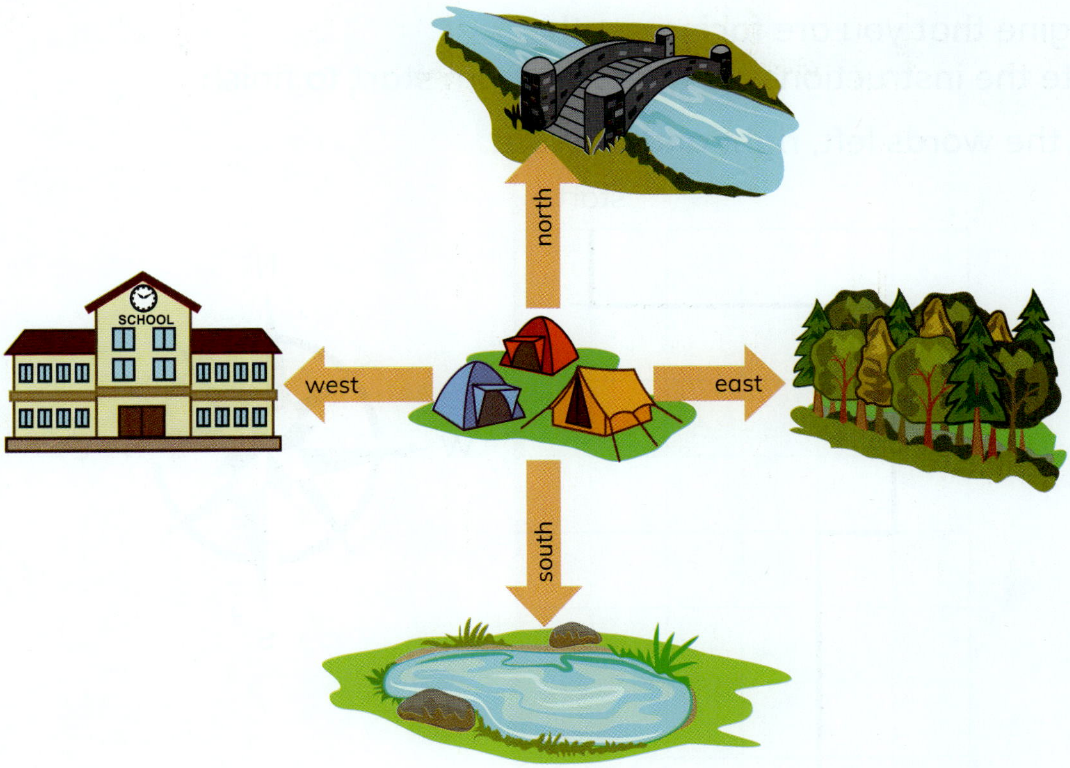

You are at the campsite.

a What can you see if you look west? ____________

b What can you see if you look south? ____________

c In which direction is the bridge? ____________

d In which direction is the forest? ____________

Now face west.

Which direction are you facing if you turn:

e two right angles clockwise? ____________

f one right angle anticlockwise? ____________

g three right angles clockwise? ____________

h Using the map, write two questions and answers of your own.

1 ____

2 ____

Will your partner be able to answer them?

4 a Imagine that you are facing south.
Write the instructions for the route from start to finish.

Use the words left, right and forward.

start

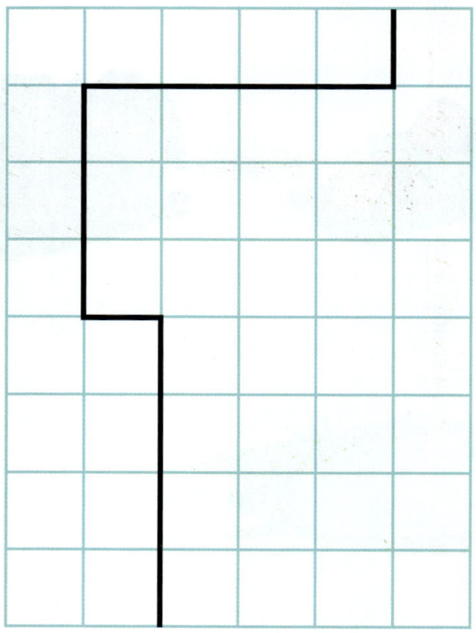

finish

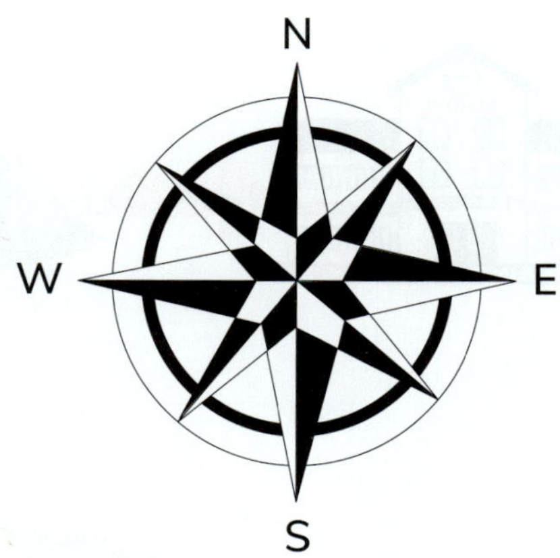

Start with: Move forward south one square, turn right . . .

____

____

____

____

b Find a different route to go from start to finish.
Write instructions for someone to be able to follow your route.

____

____

____

____

How many different routes can there be?

Think like a mathematician

Work with a partner

You will need squared paper to investigate different routes.

The hippo wants to get to the river.

Each block is one step.

Continued

It always walks along the paths and it always walks towards the river.

a How many steps east can the hippo walk before it has to turn?

____

b How many steps south does the hippo have to walk in total?

____

c How many steps east does the hippo have to walk in total?

____

d How many different routes can the hippo take?

____

e Can the hippo ever walk north?

____

f Can the hippo ever walk west?

____

g On a separate piece of paper, find a way to record the different routes.

h Investigate what happens when you use smaller or bigger blocks.

____

____

____

5 Write the instructions to get from START HERE to the school.

	School 				Play area 	
		Library 				Police station 
Bus stop 			START HERE		Super-market 	

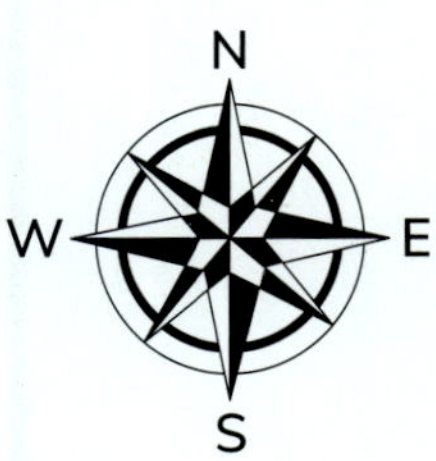

6 Stand and face your teacher.

Draw what you can see.

Turn half a turn clockwise. Draw what you can see.

Turn another half turn clockwise. Draw what you can see.

Explain your last drawing.

Look what I can do!

- [ ] I can compare angles.
- [ ] I can talk about north, south, east and west.
- [ ] I can make simple grid maps.

Check your progress

1 Count the right angles inside these shapes.
Mark them.

Continued

2 Mark the four cardinal points on this picture.

Join the dots to get to the finish.
Each dot is a step.

Move in these directions.

- six dots east, two dots south
- three dots west, one dot south
- seven dots east, one dot south.

16 Chance

Getting started

1 Draw or describe two things that are impossible (cannot happen).

2 Draw or describe two things that are certain to happen.

3 Are these things possible or impossible? Put a tick in the box.

	Possible	Impossible
A horse will grow wings and fly.		
A carrot will walk.		
A baby will cry.		
It will rain somewhere in the world today.		

This unit looks at chance experiments and shows that some things will happen, some things will not happen or some things might happen.

For example:

- With a six-sided dice you will throw a 1, 2, 3, 4, 5 or 6.
- It might rain or be cloudy or sunny tomorrow.

16.1 Chance

We are going to ...

- use the correct language when describing chance events
- do chance experiments and show and describe the results.

Knowing about chance and probability can make you better at making decisions.

If you know something about chance, you will be able to decide whether something is worth doing or not.

chance likely
might happen
will happen
will not happen

Exercise 16.1

Worked example 1

You have six dominoes lying face down on the table.

What is the chance that you will turn over a domino that has a total of six spots?
Will it happen, won't it happen or might it happen?

We can't see the faces of the dominoes, so we don't know how many spots they have.
We cannot be certain that there will be a total of six spots.

1 You have these six dominoes in a bag.

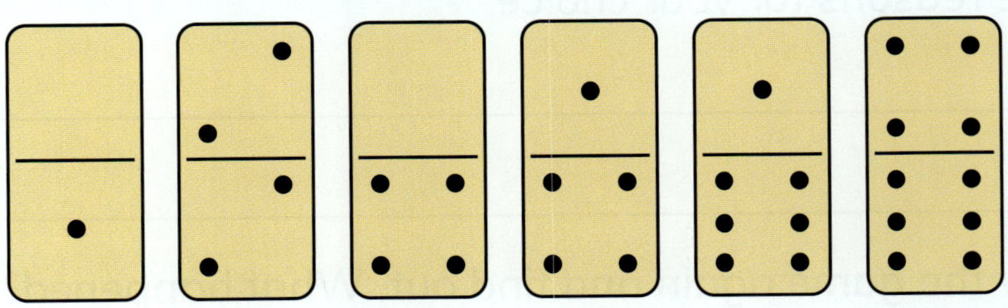

What is the chance that if you take out one domino, the total number of spots is more than eight?
Draw a ring around the answer.

It will happen. It might happen. It won't happen.

2 You need one counter and one coin.

- Put the counter in the middle of the crocodile.

- Toss the coin. If you get heads, move one space towards the head.
- If you get tails, move one space towards the end of the tail.

a After ten tosses, colour the rectangle where you have finished.

b If you play the game again, will you finish in the same place? Decide if it will happen, will not happen or might happen. Give reasons for your choice.

____

____

c Play the game again and find out. What happened?

____

____

3 You will need a pencil and a paper clip for each spinner.

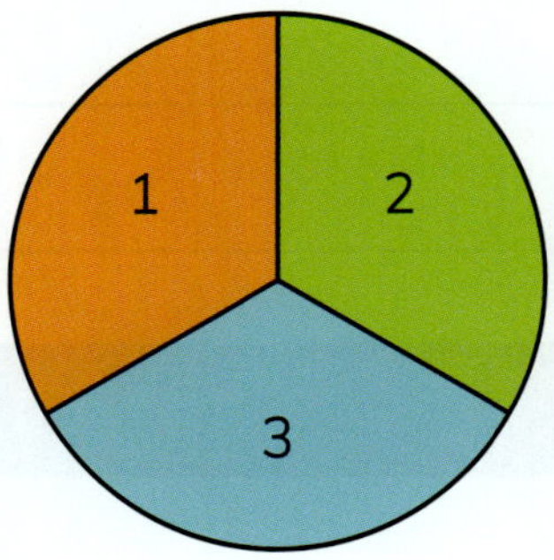

A

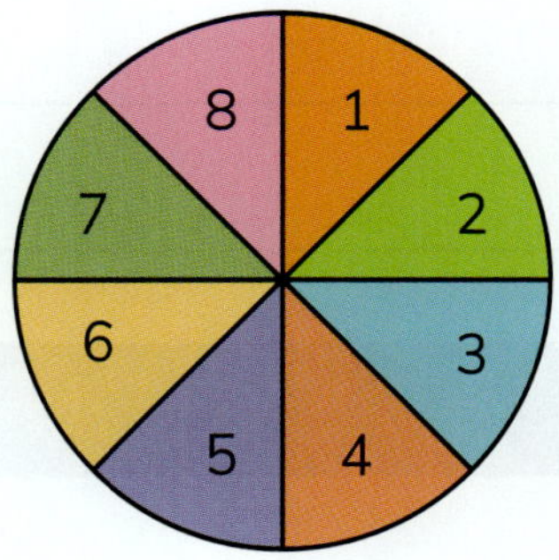

B

> **Tip**
>
> To spin the spinner, put the paper clip in the centre of the spinner. Use the pencil to hold it in place while you spin the paper clip.

a What might happen if you spin spinner A? Write down all answers.

____

b What might happen if you spin spinner B? Write down all answers.

____

c Which spinner is more likely to land on 3? Give a reason.

____

____

d Now do your own investigation. Spin each spinner five times and record what it lands on each time.

Spin	Spinner A	Spinner B
1		
2		
3		
4		
5		

e Write about what happened. Did it match what you thought would happen?

___

___

Think like a mathematician

Play this game with a partner.

You will need a paper clip and a pencil for the spinner.

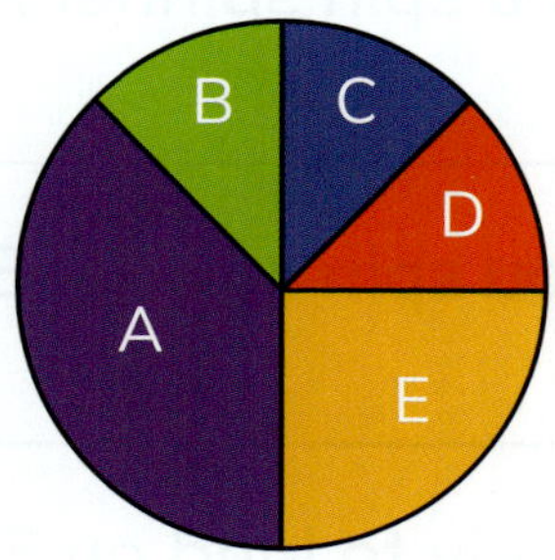

Out of 20 spins, which letters do you think you will land on? For each letter in the table, write down whether you think it will happen, will not happen or might happen.

Try it and see. Use tally marks to keep a record of the results.

Letter on spinner	Will/Will not/ Might happen	Estimate how many times	Actual number of times, as a tally
A	might happen		
B			
C			
D			
E			
F			

Talk about your results with your partner.

What did you think would happen? What actually happened? Why do you think that happened?

What would happen if all the spaces on the spinner were the same size?

Look what I can do!

- [ ] I can use the correct language when describing chance events.
- [ ] I can do chance experiments and show and describe the results.

Check your progress

1 Write the event's letter in the correct section in the table. The first one is done for you.

Will happen	Might happen	Will not happen
	A	

A You will eat an apple.
B You will meet a unicorn.
C You will eat lunch.
D You will find treasure in your garden.
E You will see a rainbow.
F You will read a book.
G A tree will fall down.

Continued

2 Place seven number cards with the numbers 1 to 7 face down.

Turn two cards face up. How likely is it that the numbers total ten? Draw a ring around your answer.

Will happen   Will not happen   Might happen

Explain why you think this.

____

____

3 Place seven number cards with the numbers 1 to 7 face down.

Turn two cards face up. How likely is it that the numbers total 20? Draw a ring around your answer.

Will happen   Will not happen   Might happen

Explain why you think this.

____

____

Continued

4

a Draw five sweets in the jar.
Use three different colours to colour them.

b Write three chance questions about the jar. The answers will be 'will happen' or 'will not happen' or 'might happen'.

1 ______________________________

____

2 ______________________________

____

3 ______________________________

____

Project 5

Venn variety

Zara, Arun, Sofia and Marcus are playing a game in pairs using a Venn diagram.

This game starts with some cards laid out face-down on the table. Each card lists a mathematical property.

Zara and Arun have the first turn. They flip over two cards which they put in the circles of the Venn diagram.

Tip

Ask your teacher for a set of number property cards and a blank Venn diagram for this game.

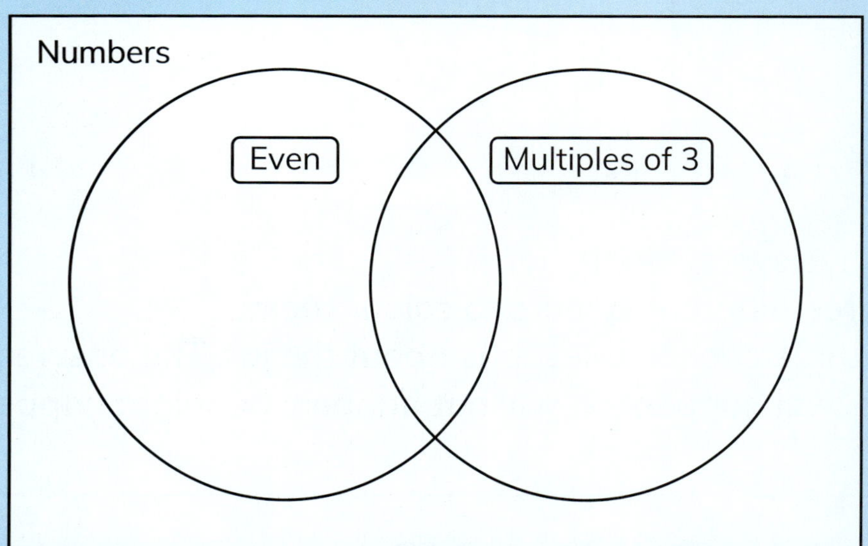

If Zara and Arun can think of numbers to put in each of the three sections of the Venn diagram, they get to keep the cards and they get two points. If this isn't possible, they still get one point if they can explain why there aren't numbers that could go in some of the sections. They then put the cards back where they got them from, face down.

Continued

Which numbers could Zara and Arun choose to put in this Venn diagram?

Can they get two points? How do you know?

Sofia and Marcus have their turn next. The cards they turn over say 'Odd' and 'One more than a number in the four times table'.

Which numbers could Sofia and Marcus choose to put in this Venn diagram?

Can they get two points? How do you know?

Have a go at playing this game, working with a partner against another pair.

Which cards can you find that would give you two points in the game?

Which would only give you one point? Why?

17 Pattern and symmetry

Getting started

1 Draw a vertical line. This will be your line of symmetry.

Use two different colours to make a symmetrical pattern.

What patterns can you see in the picture? Are any symmetrical?

17.1 Shape and symmetry

We are going to ...

- find horizontal and vertical lines of symmetry on 2D shapes
- sketch the reflection of a 2D shape.

A symmetrical shape can be split in two along lines of symmetry. Lines of symmetry will give two equal halves that are mirror images of each other.

There is a vertical line and a horizontal line.

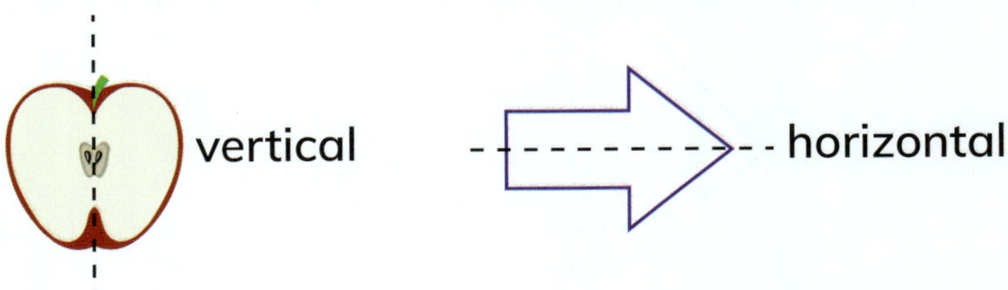

The line of symmetry is also called the mirror line.

horizontal
line of symmetry
reflection
symmetry
vertical

Exercise 17.1

1 Draw a line of symmetry on each shape.

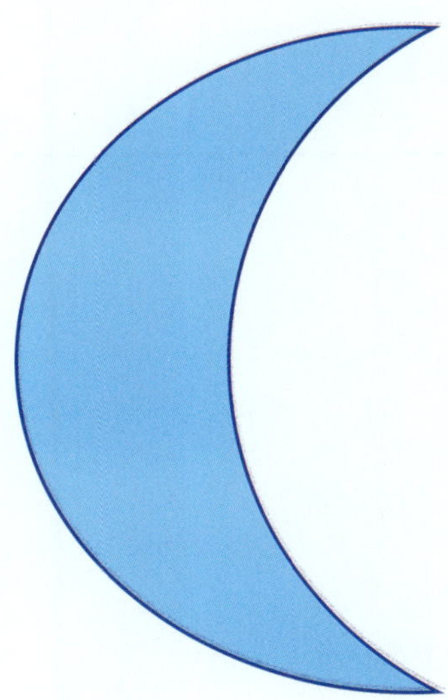

2 Sketch the reflection.

a

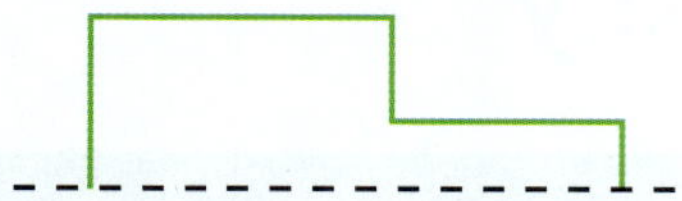

b

c

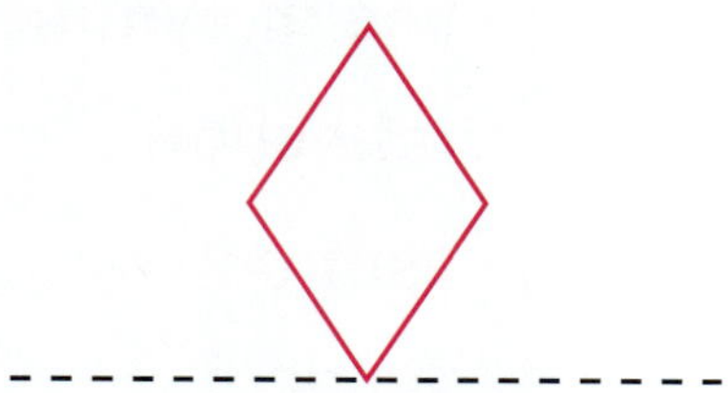

d

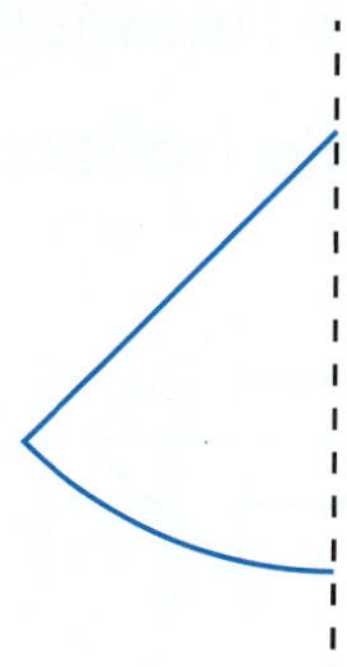

3 Sketch the reflection.

a

b

c Draw two shapes of your own and sketch their reflections.
Draw the line of symmetry.

4 Which of the diagrams shows symmetry?

a

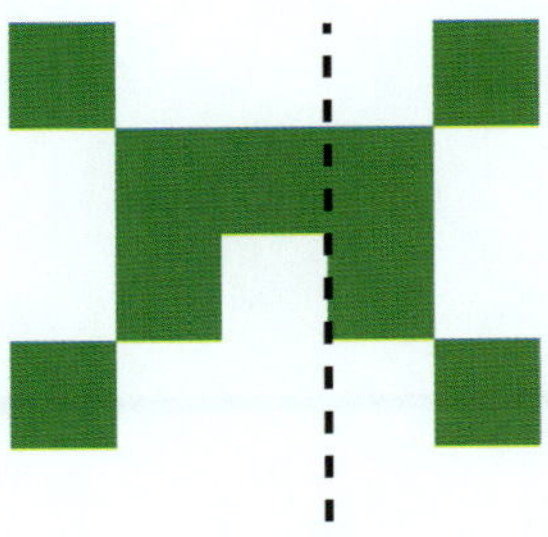

b

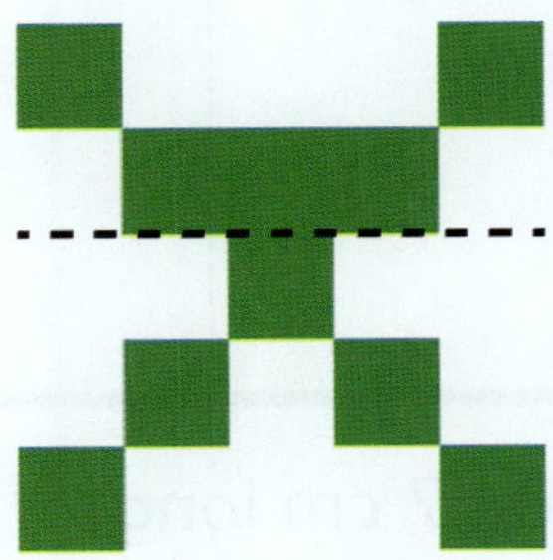

c

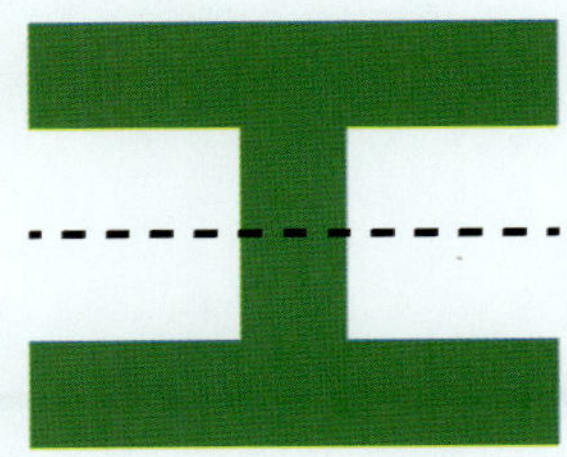

d Explain what symmetry is.

5 You have 20 straws. They are all the same length.

Use squares to draw three different symmetrical patterns that you can make with the straws. You do not need to use all 20 straws in your patterns.

For example:

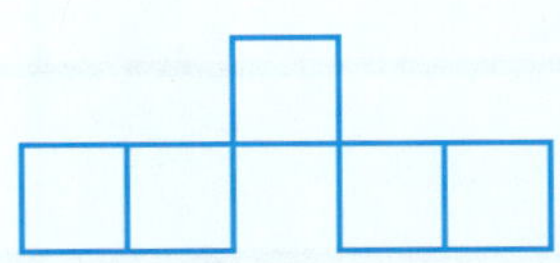

Each square uses four straws.

Draw the line of symmetry on your pattern.

6 You will need a ruler.

Follow the instructions to draw symmetrical 2D shapes.
The dotted line is the mirror line.

Draw a rectangle with two sides 4 cm long and two sides 6 cm long.

Draw a triangle with one side 7 cm long

Draw a pentagon.

7 Tick the shapes that have at least one line of symmetry.

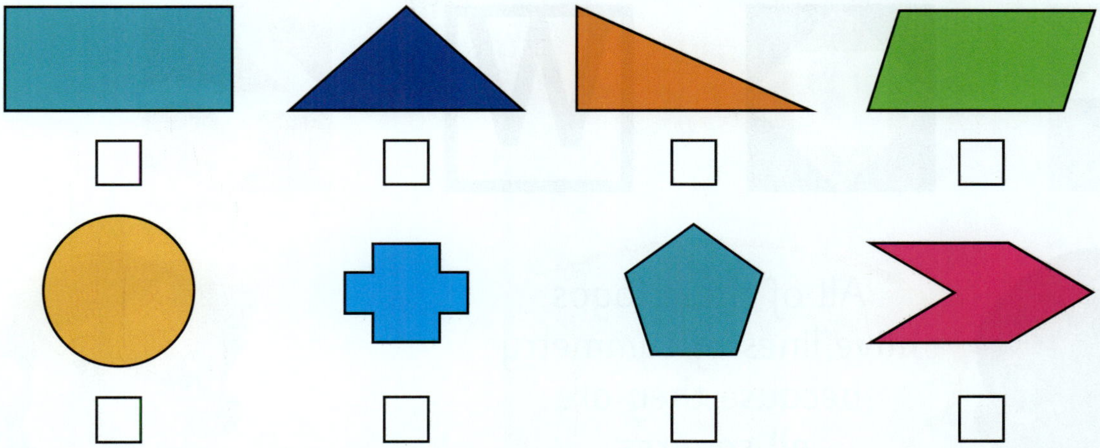

Draw the lines of symmetry on the shapes you have ticked.

Explain how you know that they are symmetrical.

____

____

8 Marcus folds a paper circle to find lines of symmetry.

Do you agree?

Discuss it with a partner.

Write what you think and why you think it.

____

____

9 Here are some logos.

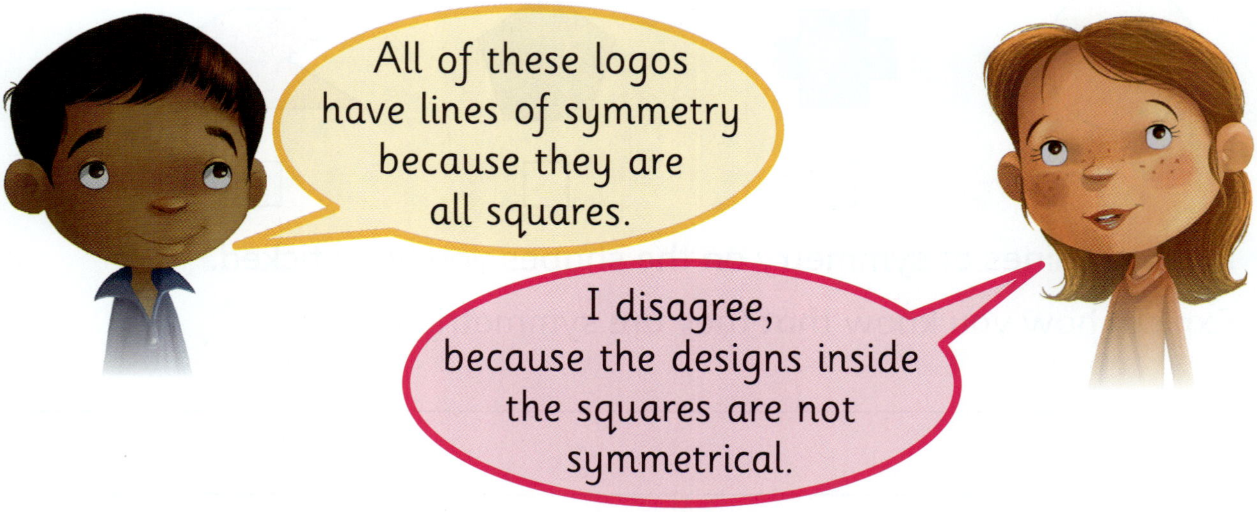

Who do you agree with? Discuss with a partner.

Write what you think and why you think it.

____

____

Think like a mathematician

Make different symmetrical shapes by folding paper and cutting out a shape. Do not cut along the fold.

Fold and cut paper to make these shapes:

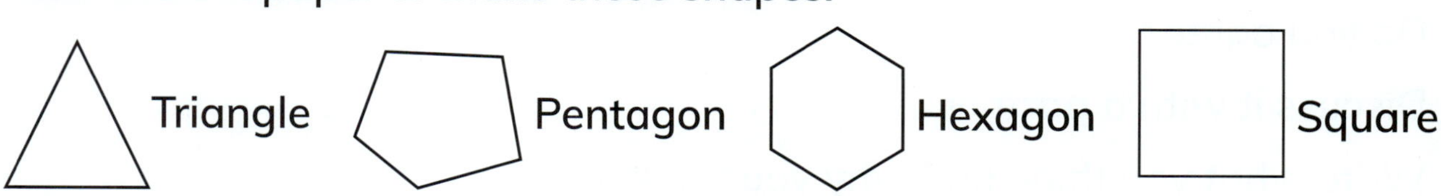

Cut two more shapes of your own. Name them.

How many different designs are there?
Have you found them all?

Look what I can do!

- ☐ I can find horizontal and vertical lines of symmetry on 2D shapes.
- ☐ I can sketch the reflection of a 2D shape.

17.2 Pattern and symmetry

We are going to …

- start with a pattern and extend or shorten it
- use horizontal and vertical lines of symmetry to recognise and make patterns.

Patterns can be made in many different ways. One way is to use symmetry.

Can you see any lines of symmetry in this pattern?

a constant extend
shorten

Worked example 1

Extend this pattern by adding two triangles each time.

This is the first step of the pattern.

To extend the pattern, we add two triangles each time.

2 triangles

2 triangles + 2 triangles = 4 triangles

4 triangles + 2 triangles = 6 triangles

We can count the shapes in each pattern of triangles to find a pattern of numbers: 2, 4, 6.

These are multiples of 2.

The **constant** is the two triangles added each time.

Exercise 17.2

1 a Starting with these three circles, three circles are added each time to extend the pattern.
Complete the number sentences.

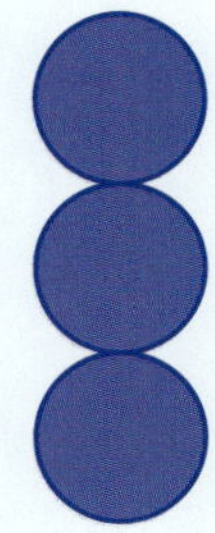

3 + 3 = 6 6 + 3 = 9 9 + ☐ = ☐

☐ + 3 = ☐ ☐ + ☐ = ☐

b How many circles will be in the next pattern?

____

c What is the constant in this pattern?

____

2 a Starting with these two squares, two squares are added each time to extend the pattern.
Complete the number sentences.

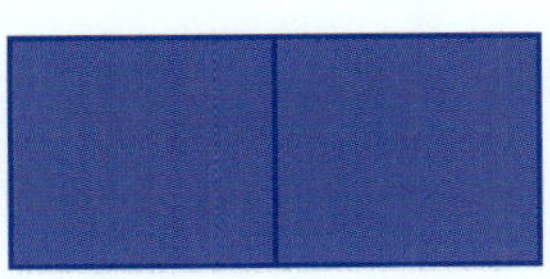

2 + 2 = 4 + 2 = 6 + 2 =

b How many squares will be in the next pattern?

____

c What is the constant in this pattern?

____

3 a Starting from this pattern of 16 squares, reduce the pattern by subtracting four squares each time.

b Draw what happens.

c Record how many squares are left each time.

d What is the constant in this pattern?

4 a Extend this pattern by adding one cloud.
Complete the number sentences.

1   1 + 1 =   2 + 1 =   3 + 1 =

b How many clouds will be in the next pattern?

c What is the constant in this pattern?

5 This pattern shows both vertical and horizontal symmetry.

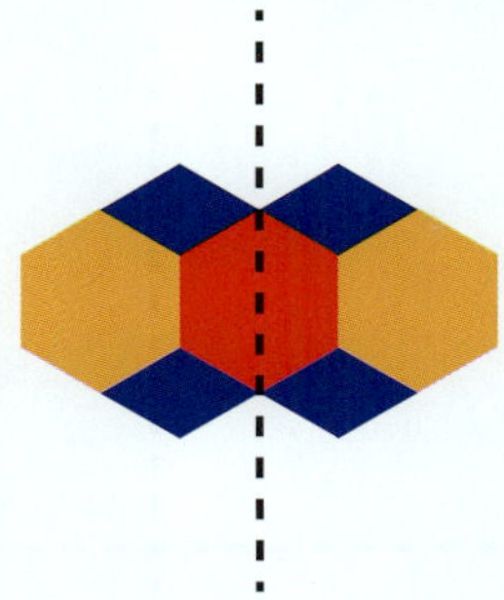

a Draw the horizontal line of symmetry.

b Use the same shapes to make your own pattern.

c Draw around the shapes you used.

d Draw lines to show vertical and horizontal lines of symmetry.

6 This pattern has one vertical line of symmetry to show the reflection.

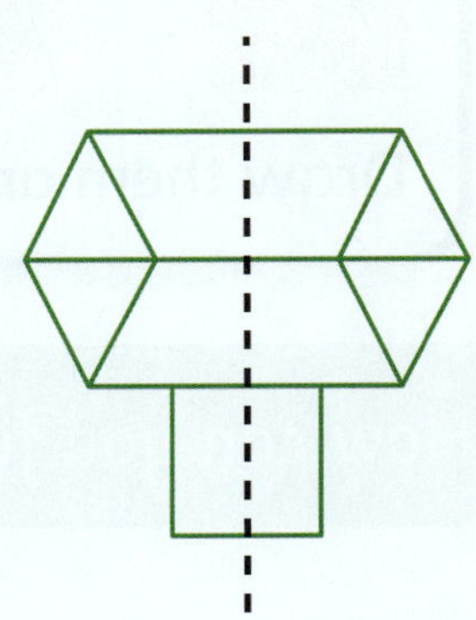

Add some shapes to the pattern so it also has a horizontal line of symmetry.
Draw the horizontal line of symmetry.

7 Use these lines as lines of symmetry.

Draw a picture or pattern that has two lines of symmetry.

Colour what you have done.

The colours must be symmetrical as well.

Does the picture look the same on both sides of the lines of symmetry? How can it be made better?

Think like a mathematician

Use these six squares to find as many different patterns with one line of symmetry and then two lines of symmetry.

Draw them and show the lines of symmetry.

How can you find out that all the ways have been found?

Look what I can do!

- [ ] I can start with a pattern and extend or shorten it.
- [ ] I can use horizontal and vertical lines of symmetry to recognise and make patterns.

Check your progress

1 Complete the shapes on the other side of the line of symmetry.

a

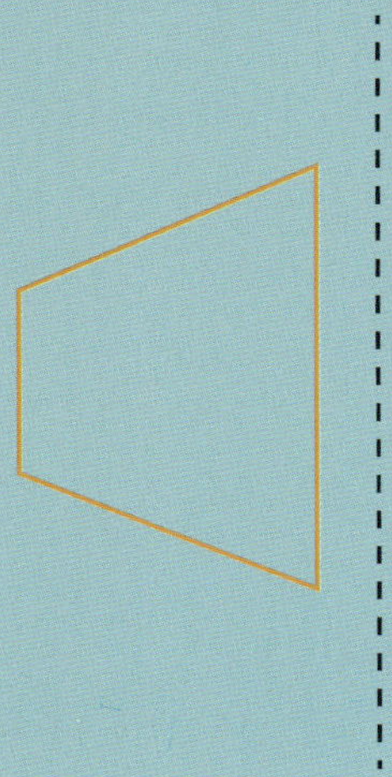

b

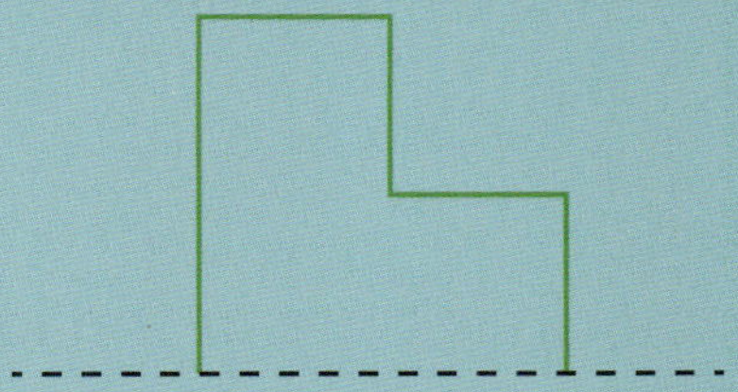

2 Sketch a shape and then sketch the reflection.

a

b

Continued

3 a Starting with these two circles, extend the pattern by adding two more circles. Do this three times.

2

b How many circles are in the last pattern?

4 Use this line as a vertical line of symmetry.

Draw a picture or pattern that is the same on both sides.

5 Use this line as a horizontal line of symmetry.

Draw a picture or pattern that is the same both sides.

Project 6

How likely?

Look at the likelihood scale.
This scale tells us the chance of something happening.

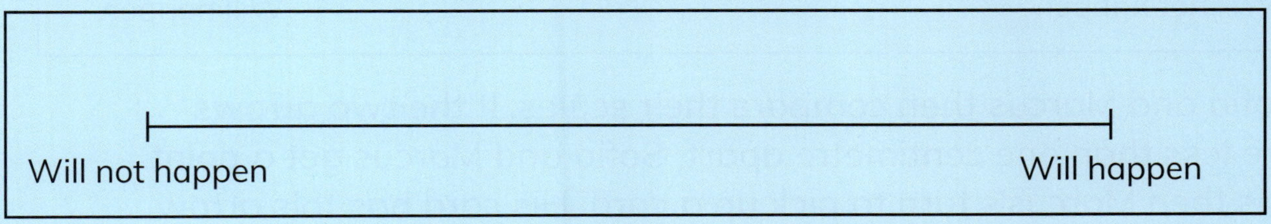

If an event will definitely happen, it goes on the 'Will happen' line on the right. If it will definitely not happen, it goes on the 'Will not happen' line on the left. If it might happen then it goes in between the two, depending on how likely it is.

Sofia and Marcus play a game using the likelihood scale.
In this game they are working together to win points.
Sofia picks up this card which has an arrow on the scale:

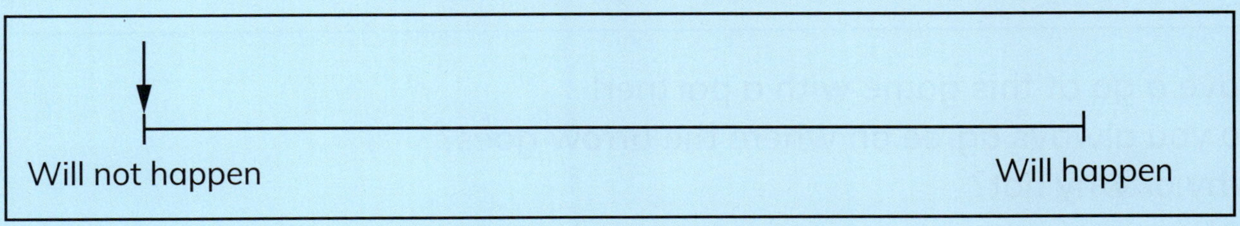

She has to think of an event that will never happen.
She says, 'I travel to school in a spaceship.'

What else could Sofia have chosen to say? Why?

Marcus has a blank copy of the scale, exactly the same as the scale at the top of this page. He has to draw an arrow on it, trying to guess where the arrow is on Sofia's likelihood scale.

Continued

He draws an arrow on his scale:

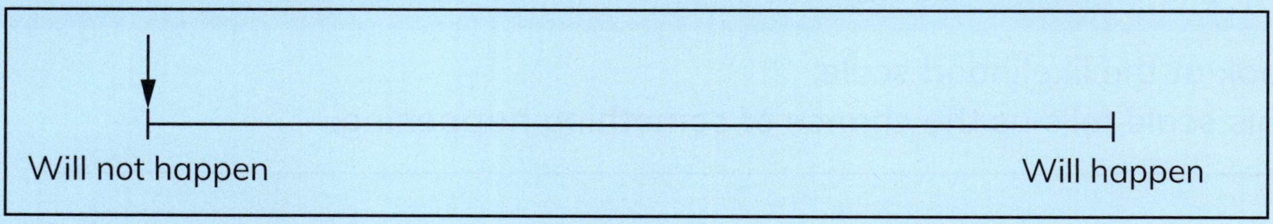

Sofia and Marcus then compare their scales. If the two arrows are less than one centimetre apart, Sofia and Marcus get a point. It is then Marcus's turn to pick up a card. His card has this arrow on the likelihood scale:

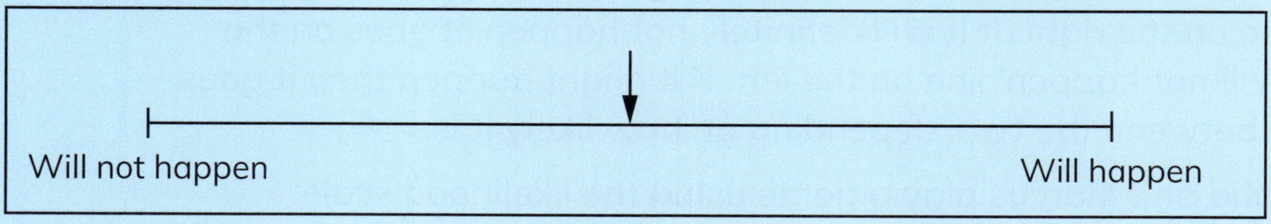

What event could Marcus say? Why?

Have a go at this game with a partner!
Do you always agree on where the arrow goes?
Why or why not?

Glossary

a constant	a fixed value or number	267
analogue clock	clock that shows the time using pointers called hands	126

apex	the highest point or top of a shape	58
approach	the way you choose to do something	176
area	the amount of space inside the perimeter of a 2D shape. For example, this square takes up nine squares. The area is 9 square units.	109

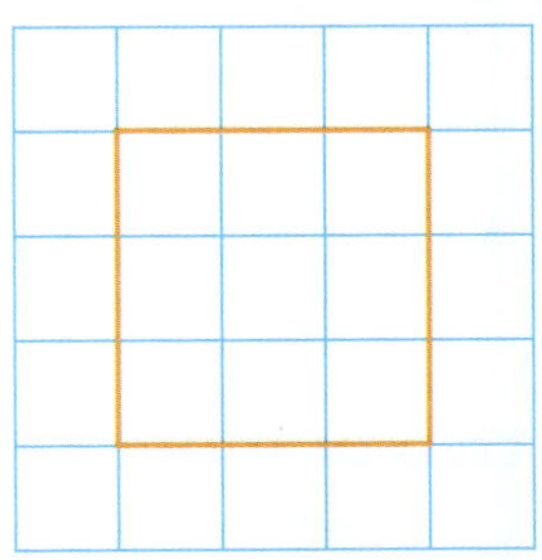

array	objects or drawings equally spaced and arranged in rows and columns. Each row has the same number of objects or drawings in it, each column has the same number of objects or drawings in it.	73

associative addition is associative. When adding three numbers, any two numbers can be added together first, then the third. 134

$7 + 4 + 5 =$ → $7 + 9 = 16$

or

$7 + 4 + 5 =$ → $11 + 5 = 16$

axes more than one axis 152

axis a fixed line on a graph 152

blank empty; for example, a 100 square with the numbers removed is a blank 100 square 144

buy to get something by paying money for it 46

capacity the total amount that can be contained 207

cardinal points the four main points of the compass: north, south, east, west 238

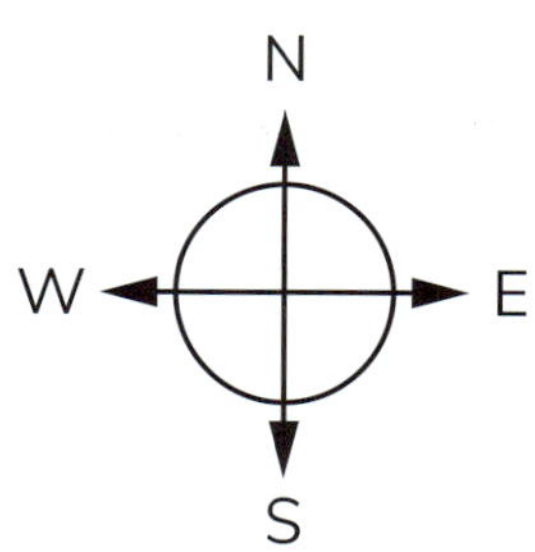

Carroll diagram a sorting diagram using two or more categories 160

centi hundred 102

centimetre (cm) a unit of length in the metric system equal to 10 millimetres or one-hundredth of a metre. We use **cm** as a short way of writing centimetre. 90

chance a possibility of something happening 250

change the amount of money left over after buying something 46

column addition recording an addition calculation in columns, with digits of the same value in the same column 134

	100s	10s	1s
	1	8	2
+	1	5	2
			4
	1	3	0
	2	0	0
	3	3	4

commutative the order does not matter, the result is the same as in addition and multiplication 73, 134, 169

$2 + 3 = 3 + 2$, $5 \times 4 = 4 \times 5$.

compass a piece of equipment that shows you in which direction you are going 238

complement how many more to make a given number. For example, 63 is the complement of 37 to 100, $63 + 37 = 100$. 144

compose put together 10s and 1s to make a 2-digit number or 100s, 10s and 1s to make a 3-digit number 38

20 + 7 = 27

100 + 30 + 4 = 134

counting stick a stick marked in ten equal sections to support counting 82

decimal point the point (.) that is used to separate the whole from the fractions of a whole; for example, dollars and cents 46

$2.50

decompose split a number into tens and ones or hundreds tens and ones 38

47 = 40 + 7

134 = 100 + 30 + 4

decreased to become less, to get smaller 192

degrees Celsius (°C) a unit of temperature on the Celsius scale 214

denominator the bottom number of a fraction, showing how many equal parts the whole is divided into 118, 184

$\frac{3}{\mathbf{4}}$

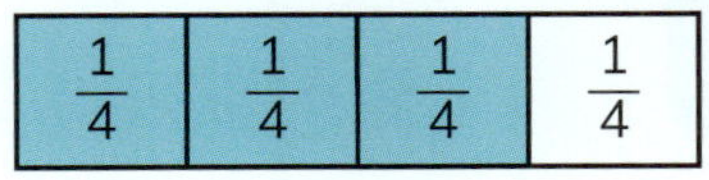

diagonal line a line drawn usually from the top corner to the opposite bottom corner of a shape, for example, a square 169

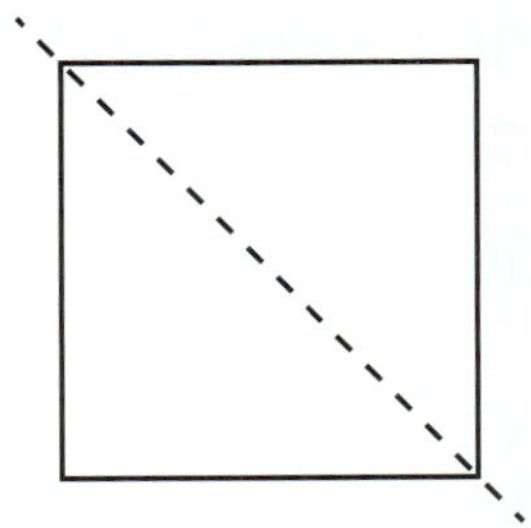

diagram simple drawing to help solve a problem 184

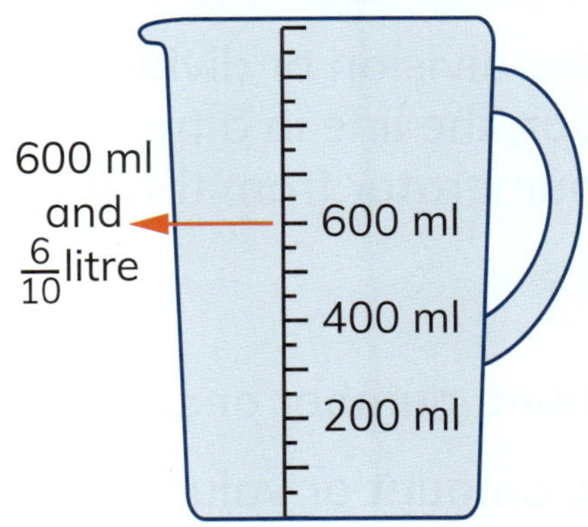

digit the numbers 0, 1, 2, 3, 4, 5, 6, 7, 8 and 9. The position of the digit in the number gives its value. 16

2<u>5</u>9

↑

the 5 is in the tens place so it has a value of 5 tens, 50.

digital clock clock that shows the time in numbers only 126

discrete data data that can be counted 152

distributive property multiplication is distributive because multiplying a number by a group of numbers added together is the same as carrying out each multiplication separately 173

$$16 \times 5 = \longrightarrow \begin{array}{r} 10 \times 5 = 50 \\ + \\ 6 \times 5 = \underline{30} \\ \underline{80} \end{array}$$

dividing line also known as the division or dividing bar, fraction line or bar, the line in a fraction separating the numerator from the denominator 184

$\frac{3}{4}$ ← dividing line

equal the same in amount, number or size 118

equivalent having the same amount or value $\frac{1}{2}$ $\frac{2}{4}$ 118

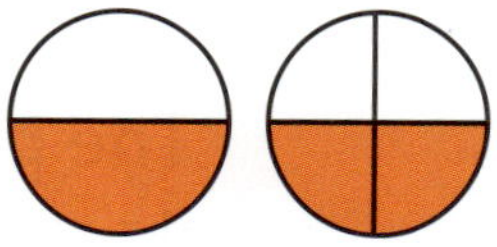

estimate a guess of a quantity or value, using what you already know 20

exchange replacing one thing with another of the same value; for example, exchange 10 ones for 1 ten 38, 140

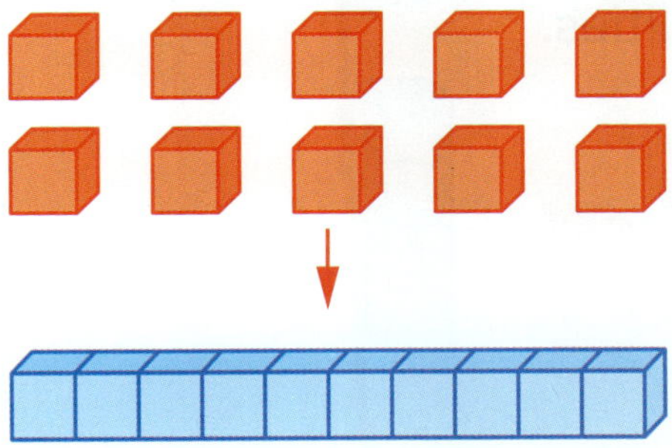

extend to continue something; for example, when you write the next three numbers in a sequence, you are extending the sequence 169, 267

fifths five equal parts of something 118

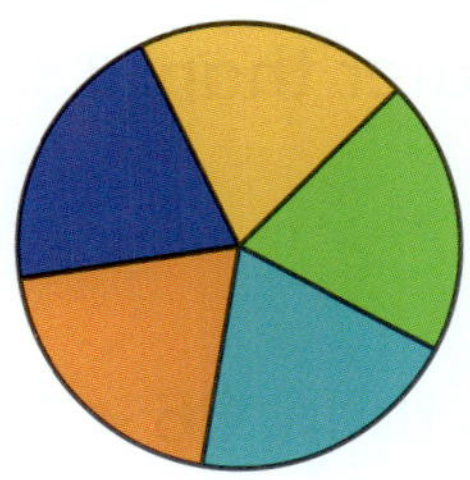

frequency table a table that lists the totals of items 26

Favourite drink	Frequency
water	7
milkshake	9

gram (g) a measure of mass. We use **g** as a short way of saying gram. 201

horizontal something that is flat and level with the ground 261

inequality, inequalities	when two values are not equal. The signs < is less than and > is greater than are used to record inequalities.  4 > 2 2 < 4	16, 188
interpret	try to understand the meaning of what is written or said	176
irregular shape	a shape that has at least one side that is not the same length as the others	102
is greater than, >	the symbol > means is greater than, 137 > 86 >	16
is less than, <	the symbol < means is less than, 86 < 137 <	16
kilo	a unit of mass equalling 1000 grams	102
kilogram (kg)	a measure of mass equal to 1000 grams. We use **kg** as a short way of saying kilogram.	201
kilometre (km)	a unit of measurement equal to 1000 metres. We use **km** as a short way of writing kilometre.	90
likely	the chance that something will probably happen. For example, 'It's quite **likely** to rain today.'	250
line of symmetry	a line where you can fold and have both halves match exactly	261
litres (L)	a measure mostly used to measure liquids; for example, 1 litre = 1000 millilitres	207
mass	a measure of how much matter is in an object	201

mentally	using what you already know to work something out in your head	144
metre (m)	a unit of length in the metric system equal to 100 centimetres. We use **m** as a short way of writing metre.	90
might happen	possible chance that something might happen but it's not certain that it will	250
millilitres (ml)	a liquid measure used for small amounts	207
minute	a unit of time made up of 60 seconds	126
money notation	written symbols used for money; for example, \$ for dollars and c for cents	46

multiple	a multiple of a number is a number multiplied by another whole number, as in the multiplication tables 5, 10, 15, 20, 25 ... multiples of 5	73, 188
non-unit fraction	a fraction with a numerator that is not 1; for example, $\frac{2}{3}$	184

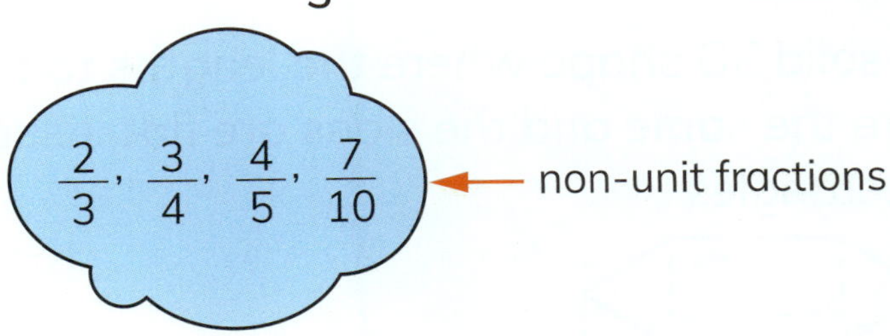

numerator — the top number of a fraction, showing how many parts you have or are being considered — 118

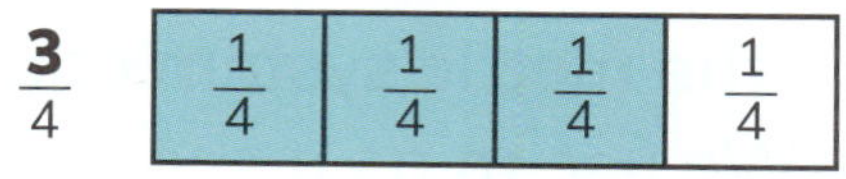

original — the object, size or cost before any changes are made to it — 192

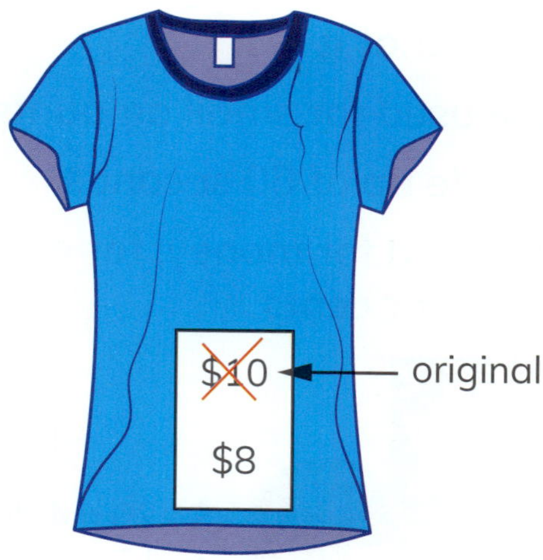

pattern — numbers, objects or pictures arranged in a regular way, so you can say what comes next — 73

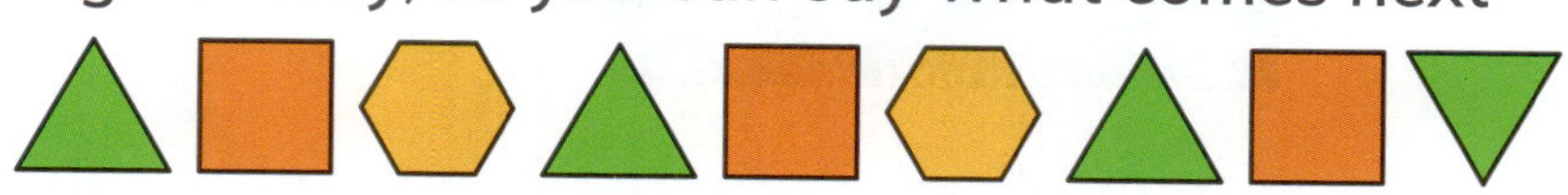

perimeter — the distance around a 2D shape — 102

polygon — a 2D shape with straight sides — 102

prism — a solid 3D shape where the lengths to the ends are the same and the sides are flat, usually rectangles — 58

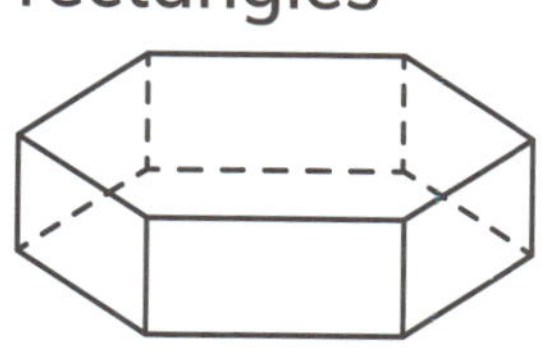

product	the result of multiplication; for example, $3 \times 6 = 18$, where 18 is the product of 3 and 6	**169**
quotient	the result of dividing one number by another. For example, $32 \div 4 = 8$, where 8 is the quotient.	**173**
range	the top and bottom limit of the possible numbers in an estimate often recorded with a hyphen in between, for example, 200–300	**20**
reduce or reduced	to get smaller or make smaller; another word for decrease, make smaller	**192**
reflection	the image of something, as seen in a mirror	**261**
regroup	put hundreds, tens and ones together in different ways, to support calculating	**38, 140**

$$\begin{array}{rl} & 127 = 100 + 20 + 7 \\ + & 118 = 100 + 10 + 8 \\ \hline & 200 + 30 + 15 = 245 \\ \hline \end{array}$$

Regroup the 15 ones as one 10 and 5 ones to find the total 245.

regular shape	a shape where all the sides and all the inside angles are equal; for example, a square	**102**
remainder	what is left over after division; for example, $19 \div 3 = 6$ r1. The r stands for remainder.	**173**
represent	to be a sign or symbol of something	**152**
right angle	an angle of 90 degrees such as in a corner of a square	**238**

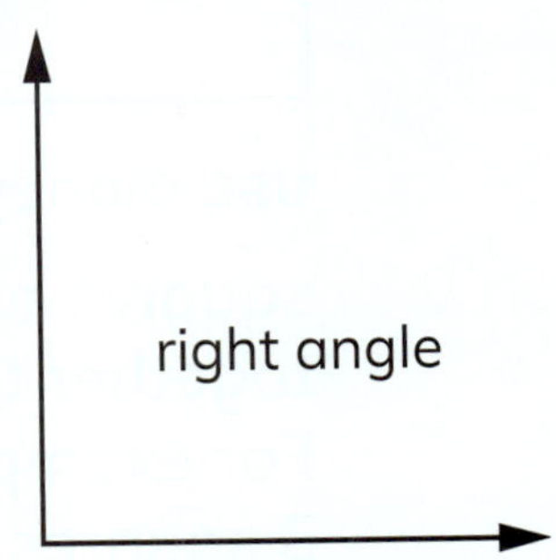

round, rounding A way of estimating. Change a number to the nearest 10 or 100; for example, 247 rounds to 200, to the nearest 100, because 247 is closer to 200 than 300. 20, 90

sequence a set of numbers connected in some way; for example, by a term-to-term rule 73

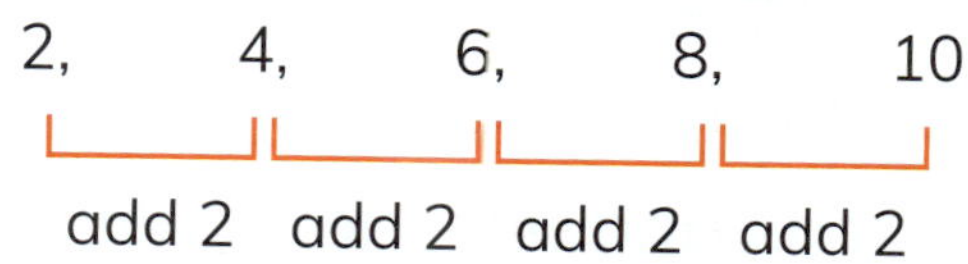

shorten to make shorter 267

simplify make easier. For example, change 14 × 4 into 10 × 4 = 40 and 4 × 4 = 16 to make it easier to find the product 56. 173

single one of something. A single-digit number has only one digit. 38

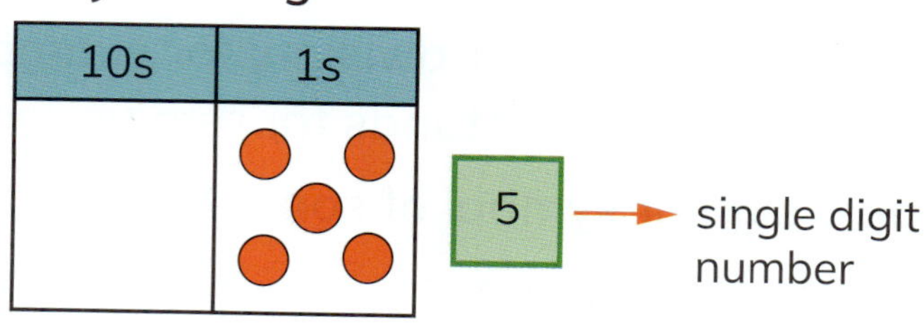

spend use money to buy or pay for something 46

square units squares of the same size, which are put together to measure the area of a larger shape. For example, this green rectangle covers 3 squares. The area is 3 square units. 109

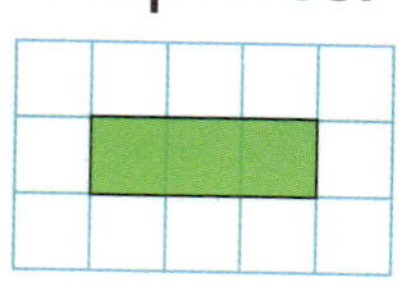

survey a list of questions used to collect data 26

symbol — a small mark used to represent something without words; for example, the symbol < stands for is less than — **16**

symmetry — a shape has symmetry if a central dividing line (a mirror line) can be drawn on it to show that both sides of the shape are exactly the same — **261**

tenths — ten equal parts of something — **118**

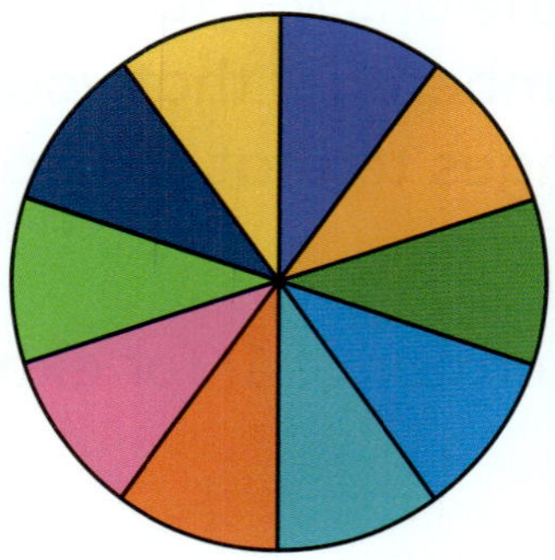

term — the name for each value in a sequence. For example, in the sequence 2, 4, 6, 8 the next term is 10, which is found by adding 2 to the previous term, 8. — **73**

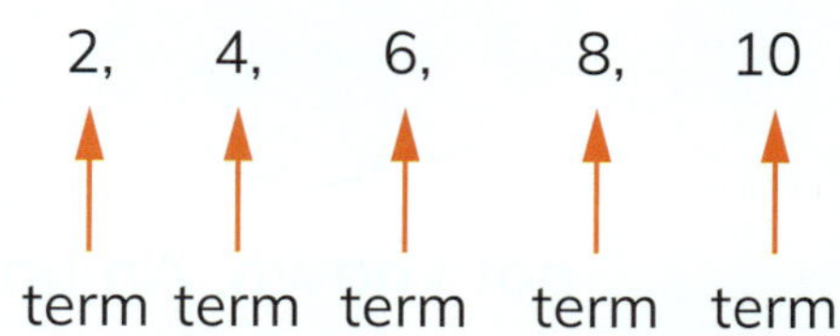

term-to-term rule — a rule you can use to find out how to get from one term to the next. For example, in the sequence 2, 4, 6, 8, 10 the term-to-term rule is 'add 2 to the previous term' — **73**

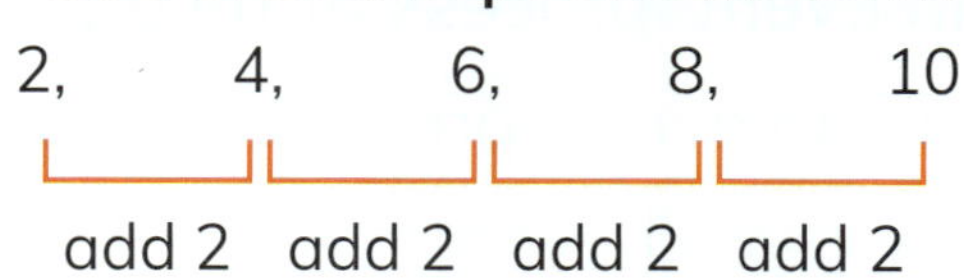

thirds — three equal parts of something — **118**

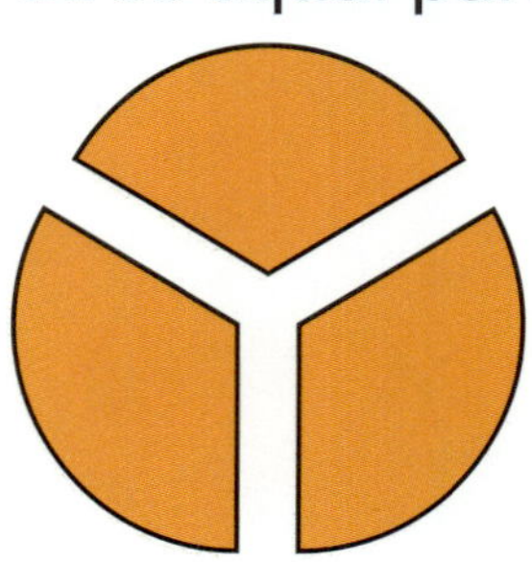

Term	Definition	Page
thousand	the name given to ten hundreds, 1000	11
time	something that we measure in seconds, minutes, hours, days, weeks, months and years	225
time interval	a period of time with a fixed start and finish	225
timetable	a list of dates and times to show when things will happen	230
trial and improvement	a method for finding the answer to a problem. Have a go using a number fact that you know, then make some changes to that fact to find the correct answer.	140
unit fraction	a fraction with a numerator of 1; for example, $\frac{1}{3}$ 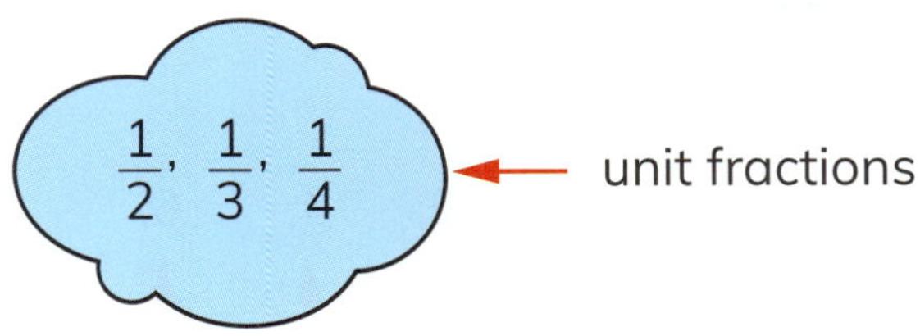	184
unknown	not known. An unknown number can be represented by a symbol, such as □, △ or something relevant to the situation.	140
Venn diagram	a diagram that uses circles to represent sets and their relationships	160
vertical	standing or pointing straight up	261
will happen	to occur as an event, process or result	250
will not happen	to not occur as an event, process or result	250

Acknowledgements

It takes an extraordinary number of people to put together a new series of resources and their comments, support and encouragement have been really important to us. We would like to thank the following people: Philip Rees and Veronica Wastell for the support they have given the authors; Lynne McClure for her feedback and comments on early sections of the manuscript; Thomas Carter, Caroline Walton, Laura Collins, Charlotte Griggs, Gabby Martin, Elizabeth Scurfield, Berenice Howard-Smith, Zohir Naciri, Emma McCrea and Eddie Rippeth as part of the team at Cambridge preparing the resources. We would also like to particularly thank all of the anonymous reviewers for their time and comments on the manuscript and as part of the endorsement process.

The authors and publishers acknowledge the following sources of copyright material and are grateful for the permissions granted. While every effort has been made, it has not always been possible to identify the sources of all the material used, or to trace all copyright holders. If any omissions are brought to our notice, we will be happy to include the appropriate acknowledgements on reprinting.

Thanks to the following for permission to reproduce images:

Cover Photo: Pablo Gallego (Beehive Illustration)

R.Tsubin/Getty Images; Martin Barraud/Getty Images; Scott-Cartwright-Photography/Getty Images; Westend61/Getty Images; John Giustina/Getty Images; Miguel Bandala/EyeEm/Getty Images; Jeffrey Coolidge/Getty Images; Yunio Baro Gomez / EyeEm/Getty Images; Stefan Cristian Cioata/Getty Images; carlosalvarez/Getty Images; Volker Schlichting / EyeEm/Getty Images; MirageC/Getty Images; Paula Daniëlse/Getty Images; Mandy Disher Photography/Getty Images; Abstract Aerial Art/Getty Images; Massimo Ravera/Getty Images; Henrik Sorensen/Getty Images; Fiordaliso/Getty Images; jamielawton/Getty Images; Suparerg Suksai / EyeEm/Getty Images; amtitus/Getty Images; Sergio Mendoza Hochmann/Getty Images; Elske De Korver / EyeEm/Getty Images; Kwanchai Lerttanapunyaporn / EyeEm/Getty Images; Huber & Starke/Getty Images; KOICHI SAITO/amanaimagesRF/Getty Images; Erik Von Weber/Getty Images; Larry Washburn/Getty Images; Peter Dazeley/Getty Images; Hello World/Getty Images; Richard Drury/Getty Images; mikroman6/Getty Images; njekaterina/Getty Images; Thatree Thitivongvaroon/Getty Images; ZargonDesign/Getty Images.